AF521761

A PICTORIAL HISTORY
Hampton / Newport News

# Hampton

A PICTORIAL HISTORY

# Newport News

By Van Hawkins

Designed by Edward A. Conner

The Donning Company/Publishers, Inc.

Virginia Beach, Virginia

Although this looks like the gang without Spanky, it's Phoebus in the early 1930's. Virginia (from left), Gene and Bill Ezell took time out to pet Hobo after tending the chickens. The chickens, pigs and a goat were housed in the barn behind the children on Chamberlin Avenue.

*Courtesy of Lucy Ezell*

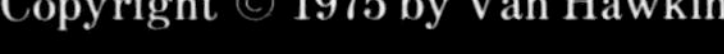

 For information, write: The Donning Company/Publishers, Inc., 205 34th Street, Suite 107, Virginia Beach, Virginia 23451.

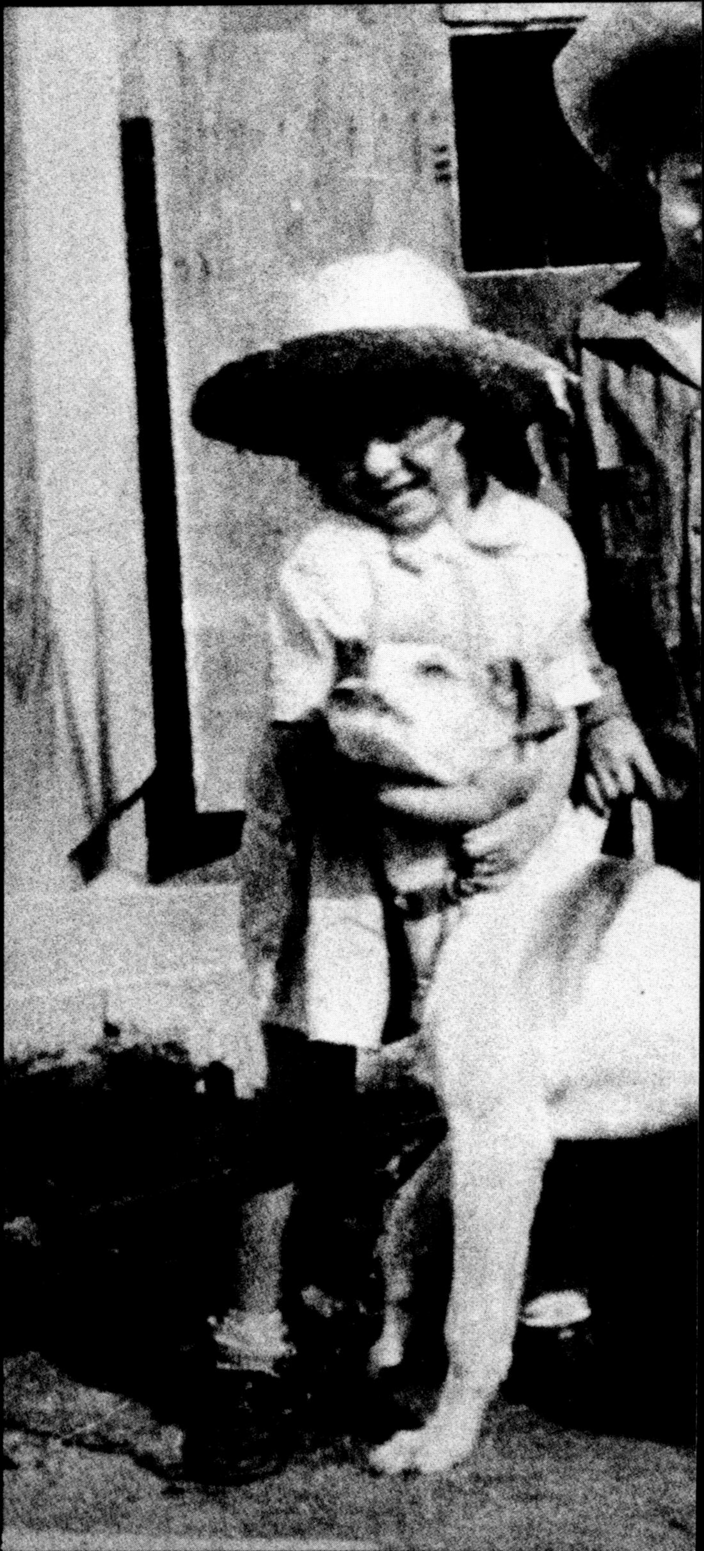

Library of Congress Cataloging in Publication Data:

Hawkins, Van, 1946-
Hampton/Newport News.
Bibliography: p.
1. Hampton, Va.--History--Pictorial works.
2. Newport News, Va.--History--Pictorial works.
I. Title.
F234.H23H38 917.55'41'00222 75-19342
ISBN 0-915442-05-1
Printed in the United States of America

*Hampton/Newport News: A Pictorial History* is what its name implies -- a history of the two cities told through pictures.

This history is not a scholarly study of the cities. Its very nature precludes this approach. For those whose demands for detail are more extensive, the bibliography will provide an interesting departure.

A look at the works in the bibliography, from which much of this text is drawn, is highly recommended to all readers. Hopefully, the limited text in this book will stimulate an interest in a more thorough exploration of the history of Hampton and Newport News.

Many details, dates and incidents had to be excluded in deference to photographs of historic and aesthetic importance. The elimination of certain material might offend some knowledgable readers who disagree with the judgment of selection. But their dissatisfaction will be no keener than the author's, who felt a sharp sense of regret as the process of selecting and discarding was tailored to practical considerations.

Readers also should be forewarned that although information has been carefully acquired and checked as completely as possible, several dates, spellings and accounts differ from source to source.

So it is hoped this history will be approached for the pleasure it provides, not the historical depth it imparts.

Van Hawkins
June 1975

# INTRODUCTION

The people of Hampton and Newport News always have had their eyes raised to the stars.

Today, members of the National Aeronautics and Space Administration are in the vanguard of those looking skyward at challenges in an infinite world; in the 1600's, travelers aboard the *Susan Constant*, the *Godspeed* and the *Discovery* studied the stars for guidance and, perhaps, relief from their uncertainty.

One can only marvel at their courage, facing the terrible Atlantic crossing with nothing but the unknown awaiting them. And one can imagine their relief when Captain Christopher Newport's ships sailed into Hampton Roads on April 30, 1607.

Several Indians watched the white men launch their small boats to come ashore. The Indians, very much in awe of the visitors, might well be credited with establishing the hospitality to strangers that has become a cherished Virginia tradition.

The Indians lived at the village of Kecoughtan, which means "great town." The settlers were so cordially received by Chief Pochin and his tribesmen that the Englishmen stayed several days before advancing up the James River to found Jamestown on May 13, 1607.

Even after Jamestown was founded, John Smith and other colonists continued to visit the village, trading with the Indians for corn and materials that enabled them to survive the harsh, early days of the settlement. The Englishmen had settled further up the James River on orders from the Virginia Company because of the increased protection the location afforded from Spanish ships.

Although Jamestown was less accessible, the colonists still wanted more protection, so Fort Algernourne was built at Old Point Comfort in 1609. The name Point Comfort derived from the comfort Newport and the settlers felt when they discovered a deep channel leading into Hampton Roads. While the fort was created to protect the colonists from European enemies, it brought the downfall of the Indians. After an inhabitant of the fort was murdered, the Indians were attacked and driven from the village on July 9, 1610, a date which appears on Hampton's city seal.

The pattern was to be repeated throughout the seventeenth, eighteenth and nineteenth centuries. The white men came, and the Indians went. Whatever the moral implications, the seed of Hampton was planted, and it would yield a harvest far beyond the wildest dreams of the original settlers.

The origin of the name Newport News has been surrounded by controversy and speculation. The most widely accepted story is that it derived from an incident involving Captain Christopher Newport. As the Virginia Company continued its efforts to colonize the Peninsula, Newport played a key role in transporting people, supplies and information to the anxious colonists.

During a trip in 1610, he encountered some settlers near Mulberry Island. They were abandoning Jamestown, but when news of Newport's arrival with more people and supplies reached the colonists, the settlement was saved. This and other news he brought from England led to the area becoming known as Newport's News, and usage changed it to Newport News.

As forests gave way to tobacco and wheat fields and houses, Kecoughtan was renamed Elizabeth City in 1619 in honor of James I's eldest daughter. Plantations continued to spring up in the prosperous area despite an Indian massacre in 1622 in which more than 300 settlers were killed. The General Assembly at Jamestown, in 1634, established eight shires, including Elizabeth City and Warwick River.

A replica of the Kecoughtan Indian Village at Syms-Eaton Museum illustrates what the Jamestown colonists probably encountered when they came ashore in 1607. A palisade of tree trunks surrounds huts, the chief's lodge, temple and ceremonial dance ring.

*Photo by Bea Kopp*

The trickle of people coming to Virginia gradually swelled to a stream, and one of the earliest and most successful colonists was Daniel Gookin. He arrived in November 1621 with men, cattle and supplies, and established his plantation at Newport News, naming it Marie's Mount to honor his wife. When Gookin returned to England, where he died, Marie's Mount was managed by his sons.

Perhaps the most notable event of early years on the Lower Peninsula was the establishment of the first charity school in America. In 1635, the will of Benjamin Syms left land and cattle for the creation of a free school. And in 1659, Dr. Thomas Eaton also willed land, slaves and livestock in order to educate those who were not financially able to afford an education. Thus the Peninsula established what has become one of the country's most honored traditions -- an education for everyone.

In 1680, fifty acres were allocated for a town to be the port of Elizabeth City County. The town was named Hampton in honor of Henry Wriothesley, the Earl of Southampton, England. An interesting sidelight to the Earl's popularity is that another of his admirers, William Shakespeare, dedicated two sonnets to him.

Much of present-day Newport News remained a rural part of Elizabeth City, but Hampton became the area's commercial center due to the many vessels frequenting Hampton Roads.

As Hampton gradually became a prosperous port town, King and Queen streets were alive with activity -- from sailors visiting "tippling" houses to planters who came to sell their produce and purchase goods. The Rose and Crown was one of the most famous colonial taverns. Dancing was a popular entertainment in the early 1700's, and provided amusement

Unveiled in 1957, this mural by Allan Jones, Jr. depicts Captain Christopher Newport's landing at Kecoughtan in 1607. The painting is located at the West Avenue Branch, Newport News Public Library.

*Photo by Bea Kopp*

for people of all ages. Many nights the stillness was broken by the rhythmic thud of shoes pounding out the jigs and reels that were popular during the period.

Hampton moved into the eighteenth century bustling with promise. John Fontaine, a young, retired army officer, described Hampton in his journal:

"October 17, 1716. At Hampton in Virginia. This town lies in a plain within ten miles of the mouth of James River and about one mile inland. From the side of the main river there is a small arm of the river that comes on both sides of this town and within a small matter of making it an island. It is a place of the greatest trade in all Virginia, and commonly where all men of war lie before this arm of the river which comes up to the town. It is not navigable for large ships by reason of a bar of sand which lies between the mouth or coming in and the main channel, but all sloops and small ships can come up to the town. This is the best outlet in all Virginia and Maryland and when there is any fleet made, they make up here and can go out to sea with the first start of a wind. There are about one hundred houses here but very few of any note.

"There is no church in this town. They have the best oysters and fish of all sorts here of any place in the colony. The inhabitants of this town drive a great trade with Maryland. They do not reckon this town very healthy because there are great mud and banks and wet marshes about it which have a very unwholesome smell at low water. There is good fowling hereabouts. We met at Mr. Irewin's where we were very merry and supped well and to bed."

Despite Fontaine's statement that the town lacked a church, the first parish in America was established in 1610 during the settlement of Kecoughtan. Known as the Elizabeth City Parish, its first church is believed to have been built on Church Creek near the present La Salle Avenue.

As the needs of the parish changed, the site of the church was moved. Records show that a second church was built around 1623 and a third about 1627 before the present structure, St. John's Church, was built in 1728.

Although St. John's later was destroyed by fire and had to be rebuilt, its original brick walls remain as a classic example of early eighteenth century brickwork.

During the 1700's Virginia produced a group of statesmen and political philosophers and leaders that would be unmatched in American history. George Wythe, who was born in Elizabeth City County and practiced law in Hampton, was one of the finest. He later signed his name to the Declaration of Independence and was known as one of the country's most respected scholars and professors.

A less reputable figure associated with the Lower Peninsula was Edward Teach. In the mid-1700's, Hampton had become a commercial center, and with so much shipping, the area was a lucrative hunting ground for pirates.

Teach, better known as Blackbeard the pirate, operated out of North Carolina in the Queen Anne's Revenge. His murderous marauding along the coast prompted Virginia's Governor Spotswood to charter two ships to find and destroy the pirate. Led by Lieutenant Robert Maynard of the Royal Navy, the ships attacked the pirate at Ocracoke Inlet on the outer banks of North Carolina on November 22, 1718. After Maynard and Blackbeard fought hand to hand, the pirate was killed with many of his crewmen. Maynard, with several prisoners, returned to Hampton Roads with Blackbeard's head fastened to the bowsprit to warn anyone who entertained ideas about the merits of piracy. The head, according to tradition, was later displayed on a tall pole at the mouth of Hampton Creek.

It's ironic that the American Revolution would reserve a prominent spot in history books for Yorktown, and yet so little would happen at Hampton and Newport News. In October 1775 Hampton militiamen and troops from Williamsburg withstood a British attack by sea, but except for occasional pillaging and minor skirmishes, there was little fighting of lasting notice. And although the revolution established the newly formed, struggling country as a force to be reckoned with, it brought the decline of Hampton as a commercial center. The inability of large ships to enter the harbor and the removal of the customs house to Norfolk led to the decline.

After the revolution, many of the large plantations were broken into smaller farms which were interspersed throughout the forests. But the area's rural tranquility was destroyed when British Admiral George Cockburn of the Royal Navy sailed into Chesapeake Bay in 1812. Hampton Roads ports were blockaded for about five months. And in 1813, Hampton received a bitter taste of war when the British occupied and pillaged the city, then continued on to Washington, D.C., to further humiliate the young nation by burning its capital.

The importance of establishing a strong defense at Old Point Comfort became even more obvious after events during the War of 1812, so in 1818 construction was begun on Fort Monroe, named in honor of President James Monroe. The designer of the fort was forty year old General Simon Bernard, who had served under Napoleon until the emperor's fall made him unwelcome in France. Bernard also

Arthur Sembler's painting depicts settlers feasting with the Kecoughtan Indians in 1607.

*Courtesy of the Hampton Bicentennial Series -- WVEC Television*

designed Fort Sumter, which would surface dramatically forty years later.

Because the guns of Fort Monroe could not command the entire entrance, Fort Calhoun, named for Secretary of War John C. Calhoun, was designed to complete control of ships moving in and out of Hampton Roads. Fort Calhoun, renamed Fort Wool during the Civil War, was located off the point on shallows called the Rip-Raps, where on occasion visiting ships dumped their ballast. But it was never completed and fell into disrepair as its value became outdated by advances in warfare.

In 1829 there were approximately 1,000 people in Hampton. In her book, *In and Around Hampton,* Margaret Munford Sinclair describes the town:

"There were four doctors to attend the sick. Two lawyers helped to straighten out matters of the town, wrote deeds and settled estates in the community. A few dry goods stores and grocery stores were also well established in the town where things needed could be bought."

When Fort Sumter was bombarded in April 1861, Fort Monroe was garrisoned by approximately 400 men, but when Virginia passed the Ordinance of Secession in May 1861, the garrison was increased to about 6,000 Union soldiers. Only about 1,400 troops were in the fort. Camp Hamilton was established at Phoebus to accommodate the overflow, and Camp Butler, named in honor of General Benjamin F. Butler, commander of Fort Monroe, was established at Newport News and extended from the bluff where Christopher Newport Park is now located to Newport News Point. Prior to the camp, Newport News consisted of two wharves, one store and a lot of farmland.

Fort Monroe was also the site of another important development early in the war. In May, escaped slaves began to trickle into the fort, and Butler declared them "contraband of war." As fleeing blacks began pouring into the fort, they were put to work and paid for their labor. Grand Contraband Camp, located near the ruins of Hampton after the city was burned during the war, became a sanctuary for the runaways.

Many people fled Hampton as the war gained momentum, and by the summer of 1861 the town was almost deserted. Then Colonel John Bankhead Magruder ("Prince John"), commander of Confederate forces on the Peninsula, ordered Hampton burned in order to prevent the town being utilized by Union troops and the runaways.

During the night of August 7, 1861, the city was destroyed by Confederate forces which included men from Hampton under the command of Captain Jefferson C. Phillips. More than 130 homes and stores were destroyed. Little survived except the walls of St. John's Church.

The most significant land battle on the Lower Peninsula during the Civil War was little more than a skirmish compared to larger and bloodier battles. Its confused circumstances give it a comic quality, yet the Battle of Big Bethel -- a resounding Confederate victory -- was the first organized land battle of the war.

In June 1861, approximately 3,500 Union troops left Fort Monroe and Camp Butler in two groups. They were searching for Confederate forces but mistook each other for the enemy and opened fire. The Confederate troops, about 1,400 men, were thus warned and proceeded to rout the Yankees.

A major naval engagement off the Lower Peninsula was to serve as a remarkable contrast in importance to the Battle of Big Bethel.

The *USS Cumberland* and *USS Congress*, big

Soldier and adventurer John Smith's energetic efforts at providing defenses against the Indians and trading for food, which he obtained from Indians at Kecoughtan, were important in the survival of Jamestown.

Although president of the colony in 1608, Smith is best remembered as the colonist saved from execution by Pocahontas. This photograph is from a seventeenth century woodcut in *Description of New England*, published in 1614. The portrait was made by Simon de Passe, one of the foremost engravers of the seventeenth century.

*Courtesy of Mariners Museum*

wooden sailing vessels, had been blockading the James River. On March 8, 1862, the Confederate ironclad *Virginia* (formerly the *USS Merrimack*) attacked and destroyed the vessels. But when the *CSS Virginia* returned the next day to attack the *USS Minnesota*, which had become helplessly aground, the *USS Monitor* was waiting. For four hours the ironclads battled until they retired, neither a victor. The historic battle, watched by soldiers and citizens from the shore, ushered in a new era of naval warfare in which iron was predominant.

Despite such auspicious beginnings, both vessels came to ignominious ends. The *CSS Virginia* was destroyed by her own people off Craney Island after Norfolk fell to the North, and the *USS Monitor* sank off Cape Hatteras while being towed south to join a blockading squadron off Charleston.

Fort Monroe never was attacked during the war. Some say since Robert E. Lee helped build it, he knew it was impregnable. Nevertheless, it played an important role both during and after the war. After the Confederacy fell, Confederate President Jefferson Davis was first imprisoned in Fort Monroe in May 1865. Charged in connection with the assassination of Abraham Lincoln, Davis was shackled, after a scuffle, in Casemate No. 2. Davis was imprisoned four and a half months in the casemate until, largely through the efforts of Dr. John Craven, he was removed to more comfortable quarters until released on bail in May of 1867.

Like many southerners after the war, the people of Hampton and Newport News returned to their homes to find barren fields, ashes where their houses once stood, Northern entrepreneurs, and property in jeopardy because of taxes. But the word reconstruction used to characterize rebuilding of the South after the war was never more appropriately used than in Hampton and vicinity.

General Samuel Chapman Armstrong was director of the Freedmen's Bureau in Hampton after the Civil War. And because of his concern about the large number of blacks who had fled to the area protected by Fort Monroe, Armstrong was instrumental in creating a school to help prepare them for the physical and social adjustments that would be necessary for their well-being.

Through his efforts, an expansive farm called Little Scotland was purchased, and Hampton Normal and Agricultural Institute was opened April 1, 1868. The school, later renamed Hampton Institute, was to make significant contributions to the Lower Peninsula's educational development.

Buckroe Beach was to provide satisfaction of a different nature. After attempts to start a silk industry failed, it was an area that underwent several ownerships. But in the 1880's, Mrs. Joseph Herbert opened the first summer boarding house, and by the turn of the century the beach was a full-fledged resort replete with amusement park, dance pavilion and "bathing" -- mixed, of course. From 1900 to 1920, special trains ran from Richmond to Buckroe Beach, bringing anxious bathers to the resort.

Hampton was incorporated as a town in 1887, and if its reconstruction efforts were arduous and frustrating, Newport News' evolution after the war was remarkable. The city was built almost overnight.

Collis P. Huntington was said to have visited the Peninsula in the 1830's as a traveling salesman. After making a fortune in California as one of the "Big Four" railroad barons who built the transcontinental railroad, his attention was focused on Newport News as an extension of the Chesapeake and Ohio from

A reproduction of John Smith's map of Virginia, issued in 1612.

*Courtesy of The Daily Press, Inc.*

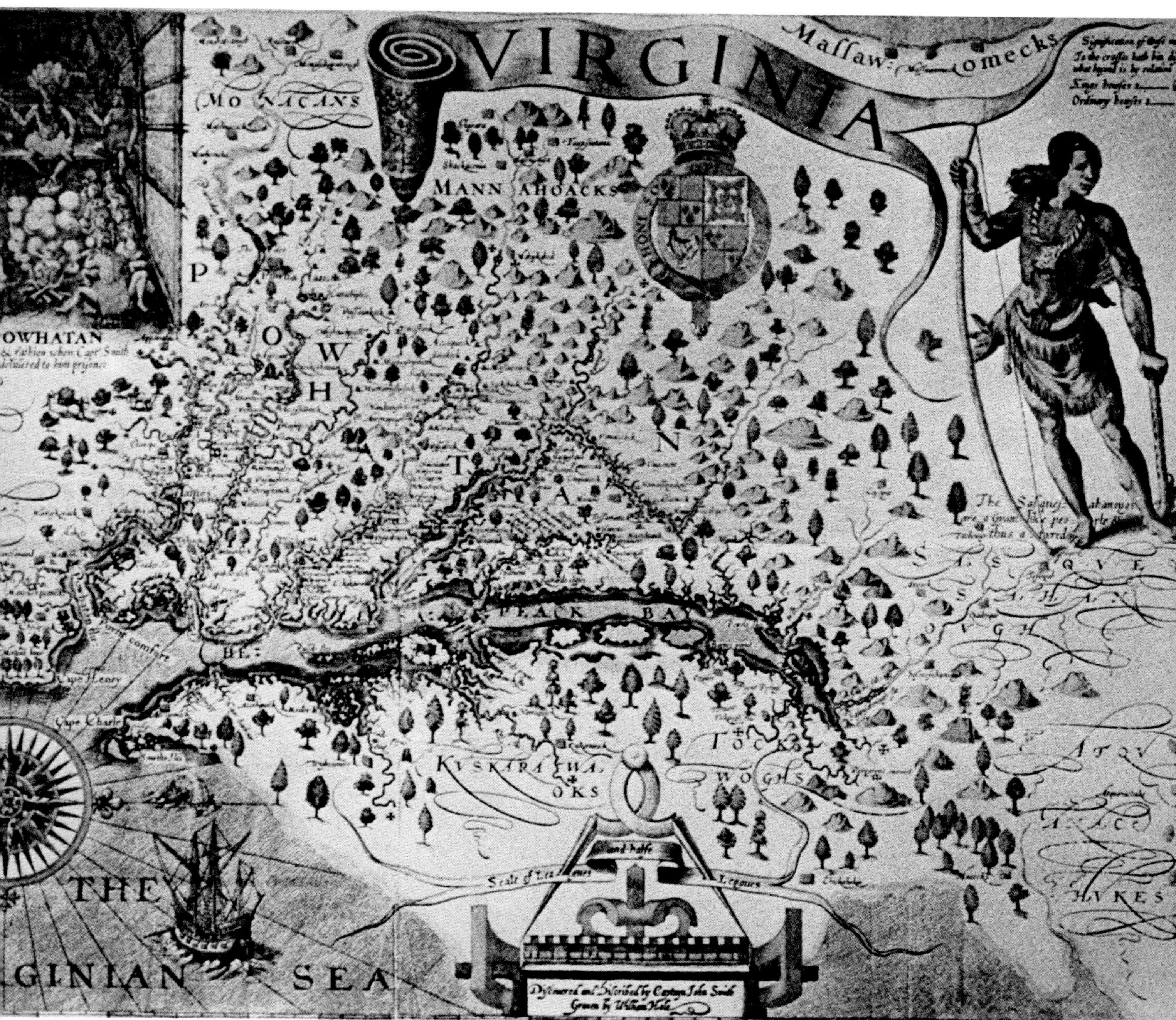

Richmond down to deep water.

Chartered in 1880, the Old Dominion Land Company acquired property needed to complete Huntington's plans, and the city was designed by Theodore Genesey. The two main thoroughfares were Washington and Lafayette (later renamed Huntington after the founder's death in 1900).

Though the Chesapeake and Ohio ran excursion trains to Yorktown for the 1881 Centennial ceremonies, regular service began in May 1882. The capitalistic visionary still was not satisfied, however. In January 1886, the Chesapeake Dry Dock and Construction Company was chartered. Dry Dock 1 opened in April 1889, and the name changed to Newport News Shipbuilding and Dry Dock Company in 1890.

As might be expected in a young, booming town, Newport News was a rowdy place to live when the city was incorporated in 1896 with about 10,000 inhabitants. Full of hard-drinking, rough workers, some areas of the city gave it a lively -- and deserved -- reputation. One of the most notorious areas was Bar Harbor (the lower end of Washington Avenue). Bloodfield's (east of 18th Street) name implies its character. Hell's Half Acre, another rough section around 18th Street, supposedly was named as a corruption of a descriptive statement by Huntington, who reportedly called Newport News "the best half-acre in the world." Hence Hell's Half Acre seemed a logical designation for such a boisterous place.

Although Newport News lost its boom town reputation as it moved into the twentieth century, it did not lose its propensity for growth. Ironically, wars have brought the greatest increases in population and housing to the Lower Peninsula. Wars create a tremendous need for military and commercial

The Jamestown colonists established Fort Algernourne at Old Point Comfort in 1609. Later named Fort George, the site became the present location of Fort Monroe. This artist's concept of the fort is based on the small amount of information known about the fort and the defenses at Jamestown.

*Courtesy of U.S. Army*

shipping, and the country has repeatedly turned to Newport News Shipbuilding to meet this need. In both world wars, the greatly enlarged labor force and expanded military facilities have had significant impact on both cities.

More than 250,000 troops were shipped overseas from Newport News during World War I. The Lower Peninsula teemed with activity as supplies were rushed through the ports.

Camp Stuart, named for the Confederate General J.E.B. Stuart, was created to handle the troops. The Victory Arch was hastily built in 1919 to honor the returning soldiers. Hilton Village, the nation's first government housing development, was constructed to help house shipyard workers. In the midst of growth problems created by war, a Spanish influenza epidemic struck the area in 1918.

Two military installations that continue to swell today's population in Newport News and Hampton were established during World War I. Camp Eustis, later named Fort Eustis, was built in March 1918 as Fort Monroe's Coast Artillery Training School. Langley Field, a joint military experimental airfield and proving ground for aircraft, was established in 1917.

After the war, the country's shipping program was cut drastically, and activity on the Lower Peninsula slowed to peacetime tranquility. An event of major importance was the opening of the James River Bridge in 1928. The bridge signaled the beginning of the end of ferries, which had been the key to transportation on the Peninsula since its beginning. Transportation by water had formerly been central to the area's existence, but the changeover was completed when the Hampton Roads Bridge Tunnel was opened in November 1957.

One disastrous event that marred the tranquility of the period between the wars was the storm of 1933. This hurricane did tremendous damage to the Peninsula, particularly at Buckroe Beach and low lying areas of Hampton and York County.

World War II brought even more activity than World War I. Again the shipyard labor force swelled. The reestablishment of the Hampton Roads Port of Embarkation, with Camp Patrick Henry set up in Warwick County to handle troops being shipped to Europe, the enlargement of Langley Field and Fort Monroe and the reactivation of Fort Eustis by the military again brought critical housing shortages. But the Peninsula's military and industrial efforts were recognized as crucial to the war effort.

Although the Lower Peninsula has gained a worldwide reputation as a military complex, particularly for the exploits of astronauts trained at NASA, it is also well known as an ideal location for water sport enthusiasts.

Residents of Hampton and Newport News are just as bound to the water that surrounds them as their forebears, but while their ancestors often relied on the water for their existence, many contemporary residents depend on the water for entertainment -- fishing, sailing or swimming.

The water still provides a living for numerous citizens. Hampton, which consolidated in 1952 with Elizabeth City County and Phoebus, is noted for its seafood. Oysters and crabs are plentiful, fish are caught year-round, and the supply is so abundant that the area provides seafood for distribution to many other cities.

Newport News, which merged with the City of Warwick in 1958, continues its role as a major port on the East Coast. Its efforts at expansion and modernization through the addition of container facilities should enable it to maintain that position.

The Lower Peninsula has also branched out from water-related entertainment to a variety of other entertainment forms. The annual jazz festival, begun at Hampton Institute in 1968, has brought thousands of people to the Peninsula in the 1970's, and completion of Hampton Coliseum in 1970 has provided a facility for everything from sports to rock and roll concerts.

As the cities have evolved in the 1960's and 1970's, with more than 250,000 residents, Mercury Boulevard has become a business and entertainment center -- with major hotels, restaurants, theaters and two new, gigantic shopping malls.

To some Americans, growth has become synonymous with everything that is bad about the United States. But growth can be planned and productive. Indicative of the nature of the Lower Peninsula's growth is that Hampton was selected as one of the nation's All-America Cities for 1972, an award given for "community improvement through citizen action."

In the 1970's, Hampton and Newport News are not without problems and obstacles to overcome. But the citizens can look to the future, like their ancestors on the *Susan Constant*, the *Godspeed* and the *Discovery*, and know they will prevail.

Henry Wriothesley

*Courtesy of Mariners Museum*

Built in the early 1700's, the Matthew Jones House became a Virginia Historic Landmark in 1969. Located at Fort Eustis, the colonial home has a Tudor entrance hall, which is rather unusual for homes of the period. The second story of the house was added about seventy years ago. The house is an example of medieval-style architecture.

*Courtesy of U.S. Army*

Unfortunately, Chesterville, George Wythe's home located on Langley Air Force Base, burned in 1910. Born in 1726, Wythe studied at the College of William and Mary, practiced law in Hampton, served at the Constitutional Convention of 1788 and signed the Declaration of Independence. Little is known about his personal life.

Later, Wythe was a professor of law at William and Mary. Perhaps his greatest legacy is the pupils he taught -- Thomas Jefferson, Henry Clay, John Marshall, Edmund Randolph, James Monroe. . . and the list goes on.

*Courtesy of U.S. Air Force*

The "Charter Elm" at Richneck Plantation is a living reminder of Newport News' history. The tree, which is reproduced on the City of Newport News seal, is the site of the first Warwick County Court. The court held sessions under the tree -- weather permitting, that is -- until the late 1700's.

*Courtesy of Newport News Public Library System*

The Old Point Comfort Light Station and lighthouse keeper's quarters at Fort Monroe were constructed in 1802. The lighthouse, with four-foot thick walls, was used by the British as a lookout point during the War of 1812. Today it is operated by the Coast Guard despite its location on Army property. The lighthouse is the oldest occupied structure in Hampton.

*Courtesy of U.S. Army*

# HYGEIA AND CHAMBERLIN HOTELS

The first Hygeia Hotel had its beginning in 1820 when William Armistead received permission from the Secretary of War to build a hotel at Old Point Comfort, but the original Hygeia was destroyed in 1862 because the building interfered with the firing of guns at Fort Monroe.

A year later, on a different site -- now the parade ground -- the Hygeia Dining Salon was built near the steamboat wharf as a restaurant. In 1872 the dining salon was enlarged into a hotel. Ownership of the hotel changed hands until it became the property of Harrison Phoebus, who made the Hygeia financially successful. After Phoebus' death, the Hygeia was managed by his family until it was purchased by the owners of the Chamberlin Hotel in 1902. It was then razed.

Work on the first Chamberlin Hotel, owned by the famous restaurateur John Chamberlin, was begun in 1890 on the same site as the present Chamberlin. The hotel opened for business in April 1896.

The first Chamberlin was designed to accommodate 900 guests, and it became one of the most popular resorts on the Atlantic Coast. When the hotel burned in 1920, 675 people were safely evacuated.

Construction of the Chamberlin-Vanderbilt Hotel began in the late 1920's, and it opened to the public in April 1928. The name was changed to Chamberlin Hotel in 1930, and it, too, was a popular resort spot.

The Chamberlin exists today, but its heyday ended with the construction of superhighways and motels.

The many stages of the Hygeia Hotel from 1863 to 1881.

*Courtesy of H. Reid*

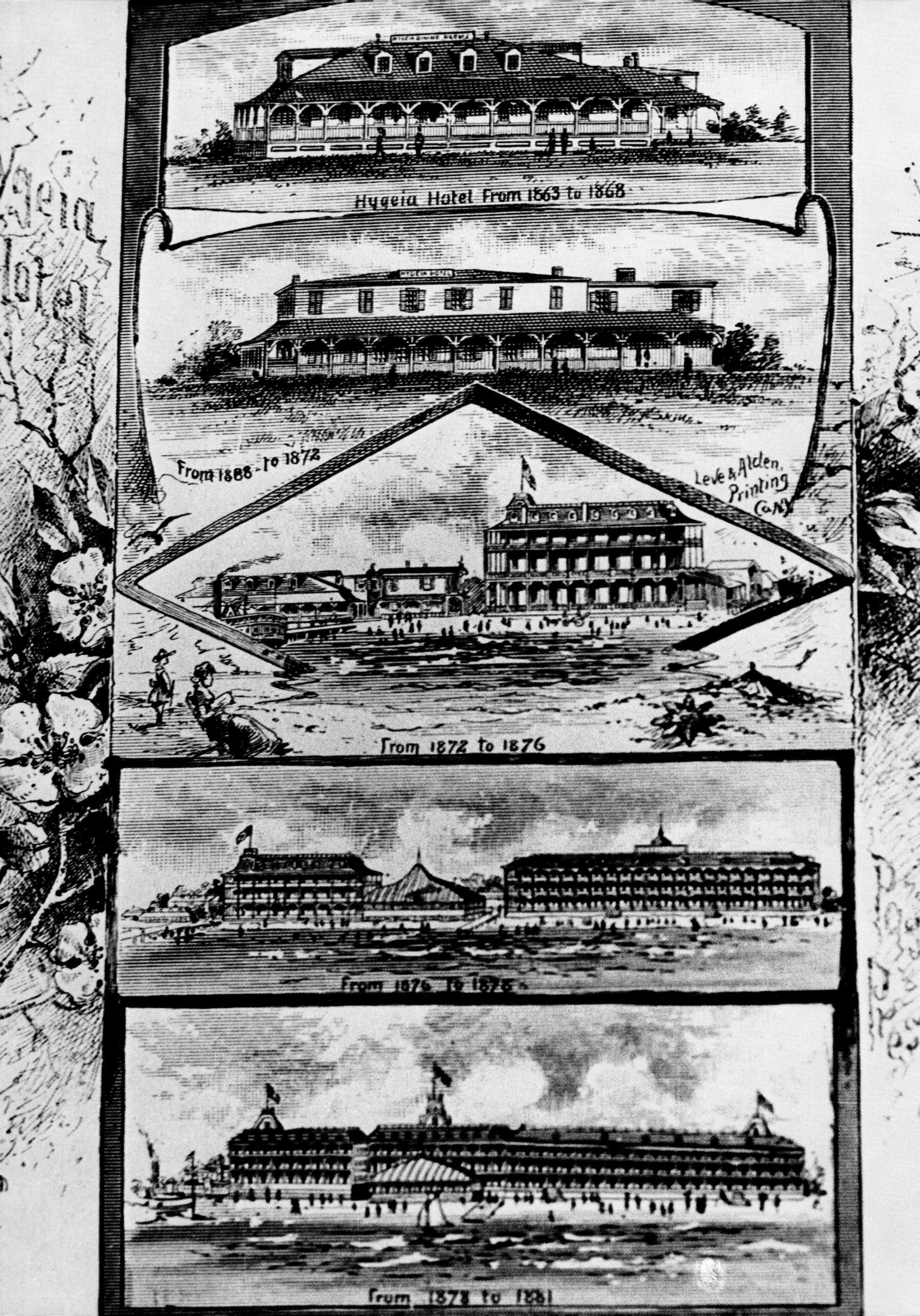

Hygeia Hotel
Hygeia Hotel From 1863 to 1868
HYGEIA HOTEL
From 1868 - to 1872
Leve & Alden Printing Co N.Y.
From 1872 to 1876
From 1876 to 1878
From 1878 to 1881
Past & Present

Visitors at Fort Monroe enjoy a sunny afternoon at the Chamberlin Hotel in the early 1900's. Note the soldiers in ranks. The parade ground (front) was formerly the site of the second Hygeia Hotel.

*Courtesy of U.S. Army*

The first Chamberlin Hotel was a popular resort in the early 1900's. At the wharf which dates before the hotel an Old Dominion Line steamboat takes on passengers. The wharf was demolished by U.S. Army engineers in 1960.

*Courtesy of Bea Kopp*

The grandness of the first Chamberlin Hotel was reduced to rubble on March 7, 1920, when fire struck the landmark building.

*Courtesy of Bea Kopp*

The site of the Chamberlin Hotel the morning after the fire illustrates the devastation caused by the fire. Fortunately, no one was killed. This view was taken from the house built on the end of the wharf.

*Courtesy of Bea Kopp*

The current Chamberlin Hotel, opened in the late 1920's, is every bit as awesome and impressive as its predecessors. These rooms overlook Hampton Roads.

*Photo by Bea Kopp*

Shirley Hogge's drawing represents one of the most famous enlisted men to be stationed at Fort Monroe. Edgar Allan Poe, serving under the assumed name Edgar A. Perry, came to the fort in December 1828. In January 1829, he was promoted to sergeant major.

Poe purchased his discharge in April 1829, a practice which was permissible in those days, taking with him letters from his officers which expressed their high regard for his services.

He returned to Fort Monroe once, in 1849, where he recited poetry on the veranda of the original Hygeia Hotel. Four weeks later he died.

*Courtesy of U.S. Army*

Born in Westmoreland County, Virginia, Robert E. Lee graduated with honors from West Point in 1829, and was commissioned a second lieutenant in the U.S. Army Corps of Engineers. After serving at Fort Pulaski in Georgia, he was transferred to Fort Monroe.

Lee reported for duty at Fort Monroe May 7, 1831. Considered an excellent engineer by his military peers, he worked extensively on the outer works of the fort, then under construction.

Lee later briefly supervised construction on Fort Calhoun. During his duty at Fort Monroe he married Mary Anne Randolph Custis in June 1831. Their first son, George Washington Custis Lee, was born at the fort in 1832.

*Courtesy of U.S. Army*

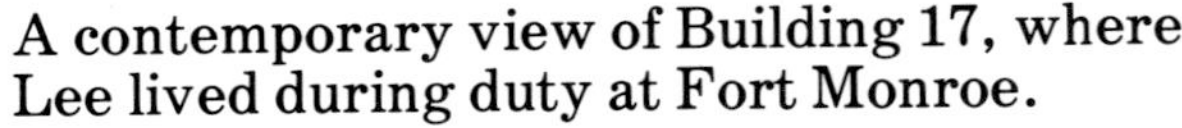

A contemporary view of Building 17, where Lee lived during duty at Fort Monroe.

*Photo by Bea Kopp*

An engraving by Edward C. Bruce in *Harper's New Monthly Magazine* of May 1859 is probably the earliest identified view of Newport News. The point was then occupied by fishermen's shacks.

*Courtesy of Mariners Museum*

This *Harper's Weekly* drawing depicts the stampede of slaves to Fort Monroe when the Civil War began. General Benjamin F. Butler, commander of the fort, declared the runaways "contraband of war" and refused to return them to Virginians who came to claim their property.

*Courtesy of U.S. Army*

Sketches from *Frank Leslie's Illustrated Newspaper* of June 15, 1861, present work and play at Camp Butler. Established in 1861, the camp ran along the present waterfront of Newport News from the bluff where Christopher Newport Park is now located to Newport News Park. After the war, General Ulysses S. Grant ordered that prisoners of war be interned at the camp. More than 3,000 Confederate prisoners were confined there.

*Courtesy of Newport News Public Library System*

NEWPORT NEWS, VA., NOW IN POSSESSION OF AND FORTIFIED BY THE FEDERAL TROOPS, UNDER THE COMMAND OF GENERAL BUTLER.—FROM A SKETCH BY OUR SPECIAL ARTIST.—SEE PAGE 74.

ENCAMPMENT OF THE VERMONT REGIMENT AT NEWPORT NEWS.—FROM A SKETCH BY OUR SPECIAL ARTIST.—SEE PAGE 74.

SECTION OF THE BREASTWORK AT CAMP BUTLER—PARTY OF THE FOURTH MASSACHUSETTS REGIMENT WORKING IN THE TRENCHES AT NEWPORT NEWS.—FROM A SKETCH BY OUR SPECIAL ARTIST.—SEE PAGE 74.

FOURTH OF JULY AT CAMP HAMILTON, NEAR FORTRESS MONROE

FIREWORKS.

2nd Regt Troy, Col. Carr.
Oration.

N.Y. VIRGINIA COAST GUARD.
FIRING SALUTES.

A sketch by J.L. Penke published in *Frank Leslie's Illustrated Newspaper* on July 20, 1861, shows the interior of Fort Calhoun on the Rip-Raps in Hampton Roads. Penke's drawing portrays the progress made in the fort's construction and soldiers experimenting with rifled cannon.

In 1833, President Andrew Jackson became so enamored of Fort Calhoun during a visit that he made it his summer White House.

But the fort, renamed Fort Wool after Major General John E. Wool during the Civil War, was never completed.

After being used sporadically by the military, it finally was abandoned.

*Courtesy of U.S. Army*

A Fourth of July celebration at Camp Hamilton is illustrated in this woodcut from *Harper's Weekly,* July 27, 1861.

*Courtesy of U.S. Army*

A correspondent from the *Philadelphia Inquirer* watched the burning of Hampton August 7, 1861, from the Queen Street bridge: "House after house and building after building melted like wax before the fiery element, and threw a lurid glare up to the sky . . . This forenoon I visited the spot again. Nothing but a forest of chimnie (sic) and walls of brick houses tottering and cooling in the wind, scorched and seared trees and heaps of smoldering ruins mark the site . . . A more desolate sight cannot be imagined than is Hampton today." This illustration is from *Harper's Pictorial History of the Civil War.*

*Courtesy of Thomas Chisman*

This reproduction of a sketch by an officer of the topographical engineers published in *Harper's Weekly*, April 19, 1862, depicts federal troops in Hampton after the burning. The remains of St. John's Church can be seen top left.

*Courtesy of Thomas Chisman*

It would be interesting to know what this man was thinking as he leaned against the foundation of a destroyed Hampton house. Taken about a year after the Civil War burning, the photograph has the Queen Street Bridge in the background.

*Courtesy of Thomas Chisman*

Efforts to rebuild Hampton after the Civil War burning didn't produce what one would call elegant results, but it was a start. St. John's Church in the background by the trees.

*Courtesy of Thomas Chisman*

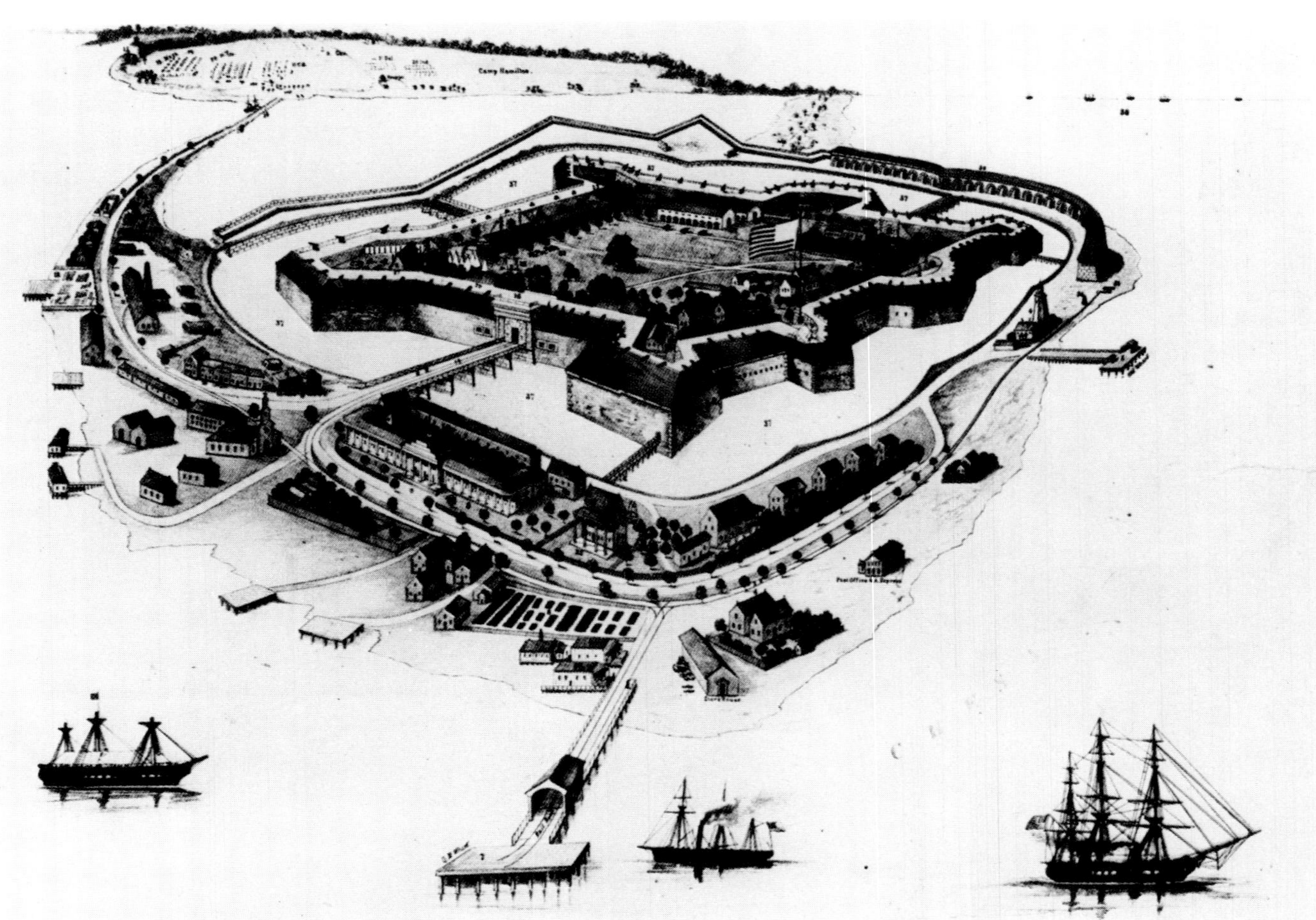


An original lithograph at Fort Monroe's Casemate Museum identifies the various buildings at the fort in February 1862. Note Camp Hamilton, site of the town of Phoebus, at the top of the lithograph.

*Courtesy of U.S. Army*

Fort Monroe was never attacked by Confederate troops during the Civil War. It is believed that since General Robert E. Lee supervised construction of the fortress he was aware of its impregnability. One of the reasons for its strength was this ten-inch Rodman gun at Water Battery.

*Courtesy of U.S. Army*

Captain Franklin Buchanan, commander of *CSS Virginia* in its March 8, 1862 battle against the *USS Cumberland* and *USS Congress*.

*Courtesy of U.S. Navy*

The South's hopes for military dominance in the Civil War rode with the *CSS Virginia* as she pulled away from Portsmouth, March 8, 1862. By the end of the day, the hopes seemed justified. Under the command of Captain Franklin Buchanan, CSN, the southern ironclad attacked blockading Union ships with devastating effectiveness. The *CSS Virginia* rammed and sank the *USS Cumberland.* The *Harper's Weekly* illustration shows the *USS Cumberland* being rammed by the ironclad. She went down with her flag flying. The *Virginia* then returned to the *USS Congress* and set her afire with hot shot. As the wooden ship burned, to explode that evening when fire reached the ship's powder, the *CSS Virginia* turned away from the *USS Minnesota,* helplessly aground, to return the next day and finish the job.

The southerners in Norfolk were jubilant, and the arrival at Hampton Roads of the *USS Monitor*, commanded by Lieutenant John L. Worden, seemed unimportant.

When the *CSS Virginia* approached the *USS Minnesota* the next morning about eight o'clock, the *USS Monitor* was waiting. The Confederate ironclad was commanded by Catesby Roger Jones because Buchanan had been wounded in the previous day's battle. The ironclads fired round after round, circling like two wrestlers searching for a good hold. Sometimes at close range, as the *Harper's Weekly* sketch illustrates, the sound of shot on metal plates was deafening. Clouds of smoke sometimes obscured the battle for viewers in small crafts and crowds at Fort Monroe. After four hours of arduous combat, the *CSS Virginia* retired to Norfolk, and naval warfare would never be the same.

*Courtesy of U.S. Army*

THE "MERRIMAC" RAMMING THE "CUMBERLAND."

WILLOUGHBY'S
BANK

When the Civil War began, Fort Monroe was seen as the key to the Union's control of Hampton Roads, so thousands of reinforcements were shipped to the Lower Peninsula. Although the fort was never attacked, readiness was maintained as illustrated by the third Pennsylvania Heavy Artillery at the fort in 1864.

*Courtesy of U.S. Army*

A *Harper's Weekly* newspaper sketch during the Civil War identifies Newport News' Camp Butler (upper right). Newport News didn't become a city until years later. Fort Monroe and vessels composing the Burnside Expedition are prominently featured. The location of the Rip-Raps, site of Fort Wool between Fort Monroe and Willoughby Spit, clearly indicated the military value of having batteries there for complete control of the channel.

*Courtesy of H. Reid*

Dr. John Craven, shown tending a patient, befriended Jefferson Davis during his confinement in Fort Monroe.

Craven was stationed at the fort as chief medical officer of the Department of Virginia and North Carolina. Alarmed by Davis' health, he was instrumental in having the former president of the Confederacy moved from the casemate to Carroll Hall, where he could be with his family.

*Courtesy of U.S. Army*

This sketch of Davis imprisoned in the casemate at Fort Monroe was drawn by one of his guards on May 29, 1865. The sketch was published in Craven's book, *Prison Life of Jefferson Davis*, in 1866. The book was important in generating public sympathy for Davis' release.

*Courtesy of U.S. Army*

When Fort Monroe's Casemate Museum opened in 1951, one of the dignitaries present was Jefferson Hayes-Davis, grandson of the Confederacy's president who had been imprisoned there. During Davis' imprisonment in the casemate, a guard drew a sketch of the prisoner sitting on the bed. In this poignant photograph, the grandson strikes an identical pose.

*Photo by Bea Kopp*

CHURCH

The history of today's St. John's Church dates back to 1728 when a church was built on the Queen Street location. It was the fourth church built in the Anglican Parish established in 1610. Unfortunately, the church was pillaged by the British in 1813 and then destroyed by Confederates during the burning of Hampton in 1861, leaving only its brick walls.

The persistence of the parishoners paid off, however, because St. John's was rebuilt in 1869 and has since then avoided the misfortunes of war.

*Photos by Bea Kopp*

# COLLIS P. HUNTINGTON AND NEWPORT NEWS SHIPBUILDING

In the 1830's, Collis P. Huntington supposedly traveled on the Peninsula as a salesman. After going to California during the Gold Rush and discovering plenty of money by selling supplies to miners, he became an organizer of the Central Pacific Railroad in 1861.

A man of extraordinary vision, he dreamed of a transcontinental railroad stretching across the United States, so he acquired control of the Chesapeake and Ohio Railway and chose Newport News for an extension of the C & O from Richmond down to deep water. This site was selected because of the harbor's accessibility and freedom from winter ice.

Once the terminus and city were established, Huntington created the Chesapeake Dry Dock and Construction Company in January 1886. The name changed to Newport News Shipbuilding and Dry Dock Company in February 1890.

The first hull built by Newport News Shipbuilding was the *Dorothy*, delivered in April 1891. From a not too profitable beginning, the company began to prosper and establish itself as an integral factor in the development of the country's naval strength. In 1907, the battleships *USS Kearsarge, USS Kentucky, USS Illinois* and *USS Missouri* -- all of which participated in the Great White Fleet of 1907 -- were constructed.

By the end of World War I, 12,500 people were employed by Newport News Shipbuilding. But as war brought dramatic increases in ship production, peace brought dramatic declines. In May 1940, the Huntington family sold the business to a group of investment firms, and the stock became available on the exchange.

Prior to World War II, Newport News Shipbuilding began construction of a radically new naval vessel -- the aircraft carrier. The *USS Ranger*, launched in 1933, was the first vessel designed and built from the keel up as an aircraft carrier. The *USS Yorktown* soon followed, then the *USS Enterprise* and *USS Hornet.* Of the seventeen Essex class carriers built during World War II, eight were constructed in Newport News.

Although peak employment at Newport News Shipbuilding came in 1943 (31,000 employees), the company has continued to prosper in peacetime largely through diversification into the production of heavy industrial equipment.

Newport News Shipbuilding also has built commercially owned vessels. In the early 1950's, the *United States* was completed, the largest passenger liner ever constructed in this country. The company has built nearly 300 ships for the merchant marine.

Since World War II, Newport News Shipbuilding has produced more than 100 ships, including numerous polaris submarines, the gigantic *USS John F. Kennedy*, the first nuclear powered aircraft carrier *USS Enterprise* and, most recently, the *USS Nimitz.* The shipyard was acquired by Tenneco, Inc. in the late 1960's.

*Courtesy of Newport News Shipbuilding*

C P Huntington

Hotel Warwick was the business and social center of Newport News during the early years. Opened in April 1883, the plush hotel and adjacent Casino and park drew crowds of pleasure seekers to dances in the pavilion, baseball games in the park and leisurely strolls.

Built by the Old Dominion Land Company, the hotel has suffered several fires over the years.

The hotel once featured a sumptuous menu, and it provided hospitality for guests such as W.C. Fields, who made the desk clerk's pencil disappear in mid-air when he was asked to sign the guest register.

The 1920's were probably the most popular years for the hotel, as shown on an early postcard.

*Courtesy of H. Reid*

An 1892 drawing of the exterior and interior of Hotel Warwick illustrates the grandness of hotels in a bygone era. This drawing comes from an Old Dominion Land Company booklet.

*Courtesy of Mariners Museum*

Beginning in the 1880's, Warwick Park (left of 25th Street) and the Casino grounds and bowling alley (right of the street) were the outdoor entertainment centers of Newport News. The area was noted for concerts, football games and first kisses. At the end of 25th Street was a pier where steamboats transported people to and from the Peninsula.

During World War I temporary buildings were constructed in Warwick Park, and after the war the park's size and popularity gradually diminished. Christopher Newport Park is located on the Casino grounds today.

*Courtesy of H. Reid*

Officials and guests assemble to witness the removal of the caisson gate and docking of the U.S. Navy monitor *Puritan* (seen beyond the dry dock gate). The dry dock is being flooded for the official opening of Newport News Shipbuilding, April 24, 1887.

*Courtesy of Newport News Shipbuilding*

In a September 1889 view of Newport News the city is hardly recognizable. Looking north from the Chesapeake and Ohio grain elevator, the shipyard is at left in the background and the Hotel Warwick at the intersection of 24th Street and West Avenue in center right. Washington Avenue is at the far right.

*Courtesy of Newport News Shipbuilding*

The commandant's residence (Quarters One) at Fort Monroe during the 1890's. Constructed shortly after 1819, the building served as the commanding officer's quarters until 1908. Among the many famous men to have stayed at the quarters are President Abraham Lincoln and General Ulysses S. Grant.

*Courtesy of U.S. Army*

The Warwick County seat of government was in Denbigh until the population explosion hit Newport News in the 1880's. The county seat was moved, and Warwick County Court House, shown on this postcard, was built at Huntington Avenue and 25th Street.

In 1896, however, Newport News was chartered as a city and withdrew from Warwick County. The courthouse became Newport News Court House, and the county seat was moved back to Denbigh.

*Courtesy of Newport News Public Library System*

MANUFACTURING SITES

JAMES RIVER →

COPYRIGHTED AND PUBLISHED BY THE

P

Newpo

COUNTY

Perspective map of Newport News in 1891.
*Courtesy of Mariners Museum*

The Timekeeper's Office and Main Gate of Newport News Shipbuilding were completed early in 1891. Located at Washington Avenue and 37th Street, the gate seemed deserted in 1895.

*Courtesy of Newport News Shipbuilding*

The award of the World's Columbian Commission at the International Exhibition (Chicago World's Fair) in 1893 honored Newport News Shipbuilding. The award was "For a model in large size of a cargo steamer, also a model in large size of the shipbuilding yard, indicating the importance of their extensive works and facilities for shipbuilding."

*Courtesy of Newport News Shipbuilding*

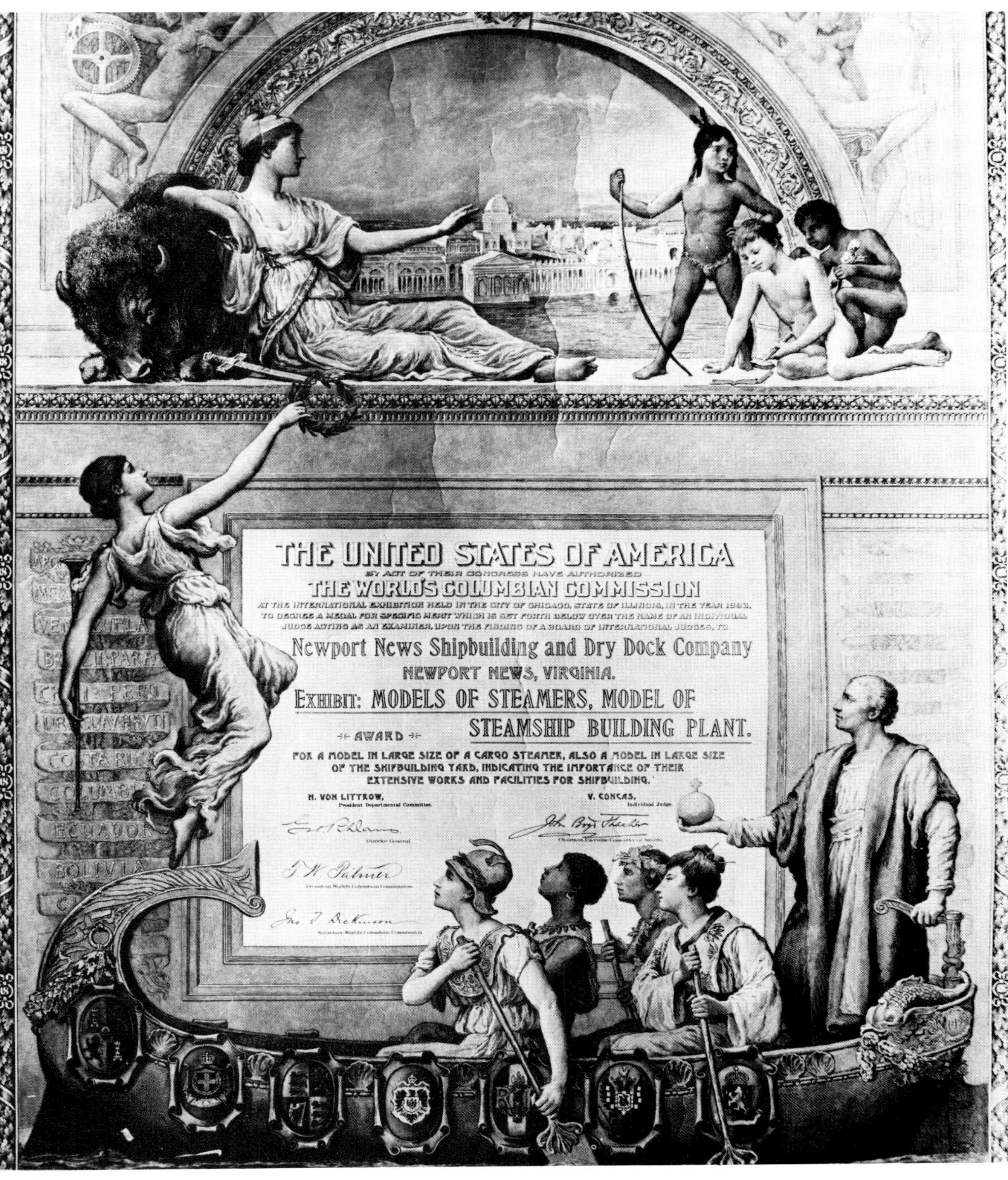

THE UNITED STATES OF AMERICA

BY ACT OF THEIR CONGRESS HAVE AUTHORIZED

THE WORLD'S COLUMBIAN COMMISSION

AT THE INTERNATIONAL EXHIBITION HELD IN THE CITY OF CHICAGO, STATE OF ILLINOIS, IN THE YEAR 1893, TO DECREE A MEDAL FOR SPECIFIC MERIT WHICH IS SET FORTH BELOW OVER THE NAME OF AN INDIVIDUAL JUDGE ACTING AS AN EXAMINER, UPON THE FINDING OF A BOARD OF INTERNATIONAL JUDGES, TO

Newport News Shipbuilding and Dry Dock Company

NEWPORT NEWS, VIRGINIA.

EXHIBIT: MODELS OF STEAMERS, MODEL OF STEAMSHIP BUILDING PLANT.

AWARD

FOR A MODEL IN LARGE SIZE OF A CARGO STEAMER, ALSO A MODEL IN LARGE SIZE OF THE SHIPBUILDING YARD, INDICATING THE IMPORTANCE OF THEIR EXTENSIVE WORKS AND FACILITIES FOR SHIPBUILDING.

H. VON LITTROW,
President Departmental Committee.

V. CONCAS,
Individual Judge.

Director General.

Chairman Executive Committee of Awards.

President World's Columbian Commission.

Secretary World's Columbian Commission.

6

In November 1893 the old frigate *Jamestown*, built in 1845, was at Pier Two of Newport News Shipbuilding for repairs.

*Courtesy of Newport News Shipbuilding*

This photo depicts the luxurious public spaces of the bay steamer *Newport News*. The steamer was completed at Newport News Shipbuilding in June 1895.

*Courtesy of Newport News Shipbuilding*

Despite Collis Huntington's claims that the James River was safe from ice in the winter, it happened in 1895. The event is such a rarity that the photographer braved high winds on a bluff north of Newport News Shipbuilding to take this photograph.

*Courtesy of Newport News Shipbuilding*

Although Newport News was chartered as a city in 1896, it still had dirt streets and a long way to go. Horse and buggy were standbys as this view of 28th Street points out. Where the trolley car is located in the center of the picture was a traffic hazard. Chesapeake and Ohio tracks crossed the trolley tracks at that point.

*Courtesy of Mariners Museum*

The first issue of the *Daily Press*, the Lower Peninsula's oldest surviving newspaper, was published January 4, 1896. Twelve days later the city of Newport News would be incorporated.

*Courtesy of The Daily Press, Inc.*

# Daily Press

VOL. I. NO. 1. NEWPORT NEWS, VA., SATURDAY MORNING, JANUARY 4, 1896. PRICE 1 CENT.


# AT THE OUTER GATES.

## President Cleveland's Door Closed to the Press.

## TALK OF A MIGHTY ALLIANCE.

**Movement to Bring All the American Republics Together. Value of the Trade of Our Southern Neighbors. All America for Americans.**

WASHINGTON, Jan. 3.—[Special.]—President Cleveland is one of the most inaccessible chief magistrates we have ever had in the White House. While it is true that senators and representatives can gain audience with him on certain days of the week few avail themselves of the privilege. This is true in part because there are now few offices to be filled, but perhaps in greater part because they do not feel that they are welcome there. Mr. Cleveland cares very little for the personal friendship of members of congress. He has never cultivated the art of pleasing them or of attaching them to himself. The result is that a comparatively small number even of the Democratic senators and representatives call at the executive mansion. When they do call, they have definite business to transact, and this is nearly always attended to in the shortest possible space of time and with the least possible number of words. The president does not encourage consultation as to the affairs of the government, or even as to the policy of the party. It is said by men who have been a quarter of a century in Washington that they have never known a president so little in touch with the leading men of his party in congress as Mr. Cleveland is. The president's idea appears to be that he can get along without personal friendships outside his immediate circle. He wishes to lead men by thought, by enunciation of principles and ideas, rather than by the loyalty born of friendly contact and mutual confidence.

**Politics In It.**

One often hears it said that if Mr. Cleveland were tactful, if he wished to be friendly and communicative to senators and representatives, if he were, in short, a leader of men as well as of thought, he would be the most powerful figure seen in the White House in generations. Probably this is true. Mr. Cleveland acknowledges his weakness, but rather glories in it. He is by temperament a man who loves to drive and who does not care to lead. He is now engaged in a somewhat bitter and acrimonious quarrel with congress. As I predicted at the beginning of the session, the game of politics between the two ends of the avenue is being played with vigor and acerbity. Each side accuses the other of insincerity, of wishing more to produce an effect upon public opinion than to secure results beneficial to the government and the country. As an independent observer, caring not a whit for the fortunes of any man or any party, but close enough to them all to be pretty familiar with their motives and private views, I am constrained to admit that in both cases the charge is not without foundation.

**Door Closed to the Press.**

Mr. Cleveland is the first president I have seen in Washington who seems to care nothing for the friendship of the press. Correspondents who have been here much longer than I have say the same thing is true of their experience. It is literally true that no correspondent for the press, no matter how able, no matter how influential in molding public opinion, no matter how much devoted to the interests of the administration, can gain audience with the master of the White House. Mr. Cleveland is the first of the presidents to close his door absolutely in the face of all his friends of the press. Moreover, it is next to impossible to gain any information at the White House. Private Secretary Thurber, while a most genial and kindly gentleman personally, rarely gives to the representatives of the press any hint of the president's actions or intentions. In all former administrations private secretaries have been useful to the press. They have helped at least their friends to correct gauging of the movements of the presidential hand.

President Cleveland is never interviewed—not in these days. The correspondent who gets an order from his paper to "interview the president for two columns" on this or that topic simply laughs and wires back without leaving his desk, "The president cannot be seen." The last time the president was interviewed by a correspondent was in the first administration. It was, oddly enough, on the occasion of the dismissal from this court of Sackville-West, the British minister. Mr. Cleveland was in New York when the sensation about the Murchison letter first became public. He was there to review a great Democratic campaign parade. On his return, late at night, he drove at once to his country seat, Red Top. Two Washington correspondents conceived the idea of driving out to see if they could not get a talk with the president. They hired a carriage and started through the rain and darkness. On the way they cursed themselves as a pair of idiots. Of course Mr. Cleveland would not see them. They would not even be able to get inside the house or past the sentries posted in the front yard.

**The Last Interview.**

But in this as in other professions one never knows when he is going to strike it rich. Sure enough, the door opened, and the two journalists were invited to seats in the parlor. In a few minutes the servants told them the president would be down right away. The correspondents looked at one another. Both were excited. How would they accost the great man? What questions should they ask him? In a few minutes the president appeared. He held out his hand to them and asked, "What in the world brought you fellows out here at this time of the night?" Then he planted himself in a big chair, and the correspondents began to feel easier. "Oh, yes; that Sackville-West affair! Well, I'll tell you about that, boys. This British minister has made a bad break. He's got to get out of this country. We don't want him here. That's plain, isn't it? What would you do, boys, under similar circumstances? Fire him, of course. But this must be done in a dignified manner. We must remember our own dignity. We can't afford to do as we would like to do—take this chap by the nape of the neck and the seat of his trousers and drop him into the Atlantic. We must preserve our dignity. Don't you say so?"

Much more did the president say, and he treated his two visitors with such genial hospitality and so completely without affectation that they drove back to Washington as fast as their horse could carry them, the happiest journalists on earth. They caught the wire and had a sensation in their respective papers the next morning.

Next day Dan Lamont said to these correspondents in his quiet way, "Good act, but I don't believe any one will interview the president again." And no one has done so.

This is to be a great year in America. Not only are we to have a presidential campaign of peculiar interest, but there is to be important movement in the field of international politics. Before the year has closed, I firmly believe, from information which I have gathered here in high official circles, there will be an alliance of all the nations of the two Americas. This alliance will be both political and commercial. Already the movement is under way, and it is one result of the declaration of the Monroe doctrine by the United States. Senhor Mendonca, Brazilian minister in Washington, tells me his government has for some time been in correspondence with other South American governments looking to the formation of a Pan-American alliance somewhat on the lines proposed by Mr. Blaine. This alliance will probably take the form of a congress to create an international board of arbitration. The real purpose is to bring all the American republics together under the sheltering wings of the Monroe doctrine.

**Our Southern Neighbors.**

Several resolutions looking to the same end have been introduced in congress, and the temper of that body is decidedly in favor of action. The proposal to bring the nations of all America into closer political and commercial relationship is about the most important movement now pending on the face of the globe. It has before it tremendous possibilities. Not many persons perhaps have stopped to reflect that in the nations to the south of us there are more than 60,000,000 people, or nearly as many as there are in the United States. There are 12,000,000 people in Mexico, 3,500,000 in the various states of Central America, 4,000,000 in South America, nearly 2,000,000 in Haiti and Santo Domingo and 2,500,000 in the Spanish West Indies, including Cuba and Puerto Rico. There are 2,000,000 more in the British, Danish and Dutch West Indies.

Surprising as it may seem, these people have a foreign trade, including both exports and imports, nearly as great as that of the United States. This is true, no doubt, because the bulk of their trade is of an international character. They do not have that enormous domestic commerce which is found in the United States, for their people neither produce nor consume such vast quantities of goods as are used by the people of this country. For this reason the foreign commerce of the nations to the south of us is surprisingly large. During the last ten years the entire foreign trade of the United States, exports and imports, has ranged from $1,314,000,000 in 1886 to $1,857,000,000 in 1892. The average for the ten years was $1,545,000,000. Against this the average for recent years of the combined foreign trade of the nations to the south of us, including exports and imports, has been about $1,300,000,000 per year. Mexico has a foreign trade of about $100,000,000 a year, the Central American states of $65,000,000, Brazil of $325,000,000, Argentina of $165,000,000, Chile of $130,000,000, Uraguay of $60,000,000, Venezuela of $35,000,000, Haiti and Santo Domingo of $30,000,000 and Cuba and Puerto Rico of $180,000,000. Other countries swell the total to the figures given. I am aware that the actual value of the goods bought and sold is not nearly as great as the statistics indicate because these exportations and importations are given in the money of the countries, which are all on a silver basis. But the total value of the commerce to and from the shores of our southern neighbors is surprising nevertheless.

**Value of Their Trade.**

If the United States can be brought into closer commercial and political relations with these countries, no good reason exists why the United States should not have a much larger share of the trade than it now enjoys. These people are nearer us geographically than to the nations of England, France and Germany, with which they now principally trade. The share of that commerce which falls to the United States is reckoned at about one-fifth of the whole as matters now stand, though we buy much more of nearly all the Pan-American countries than we sell to them. It is proposed to revive the reciprocity treaties which were abrogated by the present administration, and I understand the administration is favorable to the proposal. It is admitted by the friends of reciprocity that the treaties negotiated by Mr. Blaine did not work very well. This was due in part to the fact that those treaties were negotiated under duress, as it were. Senhor Mendonca calls it "reciprocity with a club."

The United States held threats over the heads of the Central and South American countries and forced them to come in. One nation was played against another. The result could not be expected to be favorable. Another fact which operated against the success of those treaties was the number of revolutions which broke out in the countries to the south of us and the failure of crops in Brazil and other countries. But for these hindrances it is believed the Blaine treaties, unsatisfactory in character as they were, would have shown a considerable increase in our trade with nearly all the countries. There were large increases with some countries, notably Cuba, as it was.

**Time to Strike.**

Many of the wisest statesmen we have in Washington think this opportunity one which should not be lost. Now is the time to strike out in a movement which will mean "America for Americans," not only American soil, but American trade. The ultimate consequences of trade treaties between all these nations and the United States, by which we are given advantages in their markets over our European competitors and they are given advantages in our markets, no one can foresee. But the result could not fail to divert golden streams of commerce from Europe to the United States and to open up markets of prime importance.

If to this general union of the republics of all the Americas should be added independence of Cuba and the creation of another great American republic, cutting loose from the monetary and commercial domination of the old world, the value of the new arrangement would be greatly enhanced, for Cuba's foreign trade is peculiarly rich and desirable. I have information which leads me to the hope, if not to the belief, that this will occur during the present year. After Venezuela, Cuba. Mark the prediction.

WALTER WELLMAN.

## LITTLE KENTUCKY.

**It May Some Day Be Claimed as a Part of Tennessee.**

Little Kentucky, as it might be dubbed very appropriately, is located opposite Island No. 10, where Kentucky and Tennessee meet. The river, by gradually cutting out the Kentucky bank, had worn off a narrow strip of land, until one bright morning several people who lived on this side of the line woke up to find themselves on the other side. In other words, the swift current had washed away the neck of earth which made the extreme southwestern corner of this state a part of the commonwealth of Kentucky. The section of territory thus separated from its parent, as it were, is ten miles long and five miles wide—quite a good mouthful to take in at one bite, even for the greedy Mississippi.

Every well posted river man and every person who is acquainted with the geography and topography of this state will understand how such a thing could happen. Right at the state line the river forms a loop about ten miles long. The loop extends up into Fulton county. The swift stream has simply drawn this noose tight and formed an island out of what was formerly a peninsula. Hickman is the closest town of any size to the place where all this landmaking occurred. Darnell, a little hamlet over in Obion county, Tenn., is quite near the spot.

The boundary line between Kentucky and Tennessee has always been rather complicated down about Island No. 10, owing to the peculiar bend in the Mississippi mentioned above. The lakes, bayous and sloughs which bisect that corner of Fulton county in all directions also serve to mix matters. The biting off of such a large strip of soil will add to the general confusion, and the question may arise as to whether Little Kentucky will hereafter belong to the domain of the Volunteer State or still be a part and parcel of the dark and bloody ground.—Paducah News.

**Freeman's Sensitiveness.**

One incident of Freeman's early life preserved by Mr. Stephens is thoroughly characteristic. Before he was of age he was in love, and as soon as he reached 21 he offered marriage and was accepted. Some opposition from Freeman's own kinsfolk seemed the only hindrance to a happy union. But another was created by the sensitiveness of Freeman's own conscience. "He had expectations of a sufficient income, but it was partly derived from coal mines, and the shocking disclosures recently made respecting the treatment of colliers made him doubt whether he could conscientiously draw an income from that branch of industry until the system was reformed." There we see the same temper at work which in later days made Freeman throw up a pleasant and lucrative connection with The Saturday Review because he disapproved of its foreign politics. His standard of right and wrong might sometimes be perverse, his judgments hastily formed, but seldom has any man lived to whom the call of duty, once made clear, was more absolutely imperative, in defiance of any pleas of convenience or of usage. His action was always in purpose the embodiment of George Eliot's fine lines:

Nay, falter not. 'Tis an assured good
To seek the noblest; 'tis your only good
Now you have seen it, for that higher vision
Poisons all meaner choice for evermore.

—Quarterly Review.

**People Who Eat Hair.**

It is difficult to imagine people eating hair, but there are many, especially girls and young women, who do so, as experience proves. Doctors conducting post mortem examinations have been surprised to find a large quantity of hair in the stomach of the deceased person.

Not long ago an English medical man found as much as four pounds of hair in the stomach of a woman about 30 years old, and similar cases have been officially reported from various parts of the world.

Dr. Swaim lately performed an operation for tumor, when, to his astonishment, the cause of complaint was a mass of hair weighing between four and five pounds.

In this case the patient confessed that she had contracted a habit of biting off the ends of her hair, just as some bite their finger nails.—Pearson's Weekly.

**Three Strange and Remarkable Men.**

As Dumas, the grandfather, prided himself more upon his wonderful strength and skill in athletics than his generalship; as Dumas, the second, prided himself more upon his knowledge of cookery than the authorship of "The Three Musketeers," so Dumas, the third, prided himself more upon his knowledge of art than upon the writing of "La Dame aux Camelias." They were three strange and remarkable men.

# CHESAPEAKE AND OHIO.

## Biggest Year in the History of This End of the Line.

## A GREAT RAILWAY SYSTEM.

**Its Transatlantic Steamship Line a Gratifying Success. Immense Amount of Freight Exported Monthly. Large Inward Cargoes. Chartered Steamers.**

The fact that the Chesapeake & Ohio Railway Company is arranging to build a magnificent passenger depot in Richmond has been the subject of several newspaper articles and has attracted a great deal of favorable comment in railroad circles and among people in general. While the enterprise of the company as evidenced by its decision to build such a superb structure is being discussed, it will be of interest to the public to know something of the immense business of this great railway system in Newport News.

Last year's traffic of the company at this port was heavier than ever before in the history of the road, and the month of December surpassed all previous months in the volume of freight handled. The six steamers owned by the Chesadeake & Ohio Steamship Company ran between Newport News and London and Liverpool as regularly as ferryboats, carrying very large outward cargoes and gradually increasing inward cargoes. The export business of the line was so heavy during the year that the regular line was augmented by several chartered steamships. The exports by the regular line alone amounted to about 15,000 tons a month and the imports to 5,000 tons a month. It has not been long since the Hamburg-American line steamers began to make semi-monthly trips between Newpsrt News and Hamburg, yet the business of the new line has grown to large proportions. The steamship Albano, of this line, sailed Tuesday morning with the largest cargo ever shipped from this port to Hamburg. It consisted of 300 cars or 4,000 tons of miscellaneous freight. This line has a close traffic alliance with the Chesapeake & Ohio railway, and the arrangement has been a very satisfactory one to both companies.

MR. H. E. PARKER, TERMINAL SUPERINTENDENT OF THE C. & O. RY.

Some idea may be gained as to the enormous business of the Chesapeake & Ohio railway at this point when it is stated that eight large steamships were being loaded with foreign cargoes here Tuesday at the same time. Three of these vessels took full cargoes of grain and the others carried miscellaneous merchandise. During the last three working days of 1895 there were about half a million bushels of grain transferred from the C. & O. elevator into foreign bound vessels. In addition to the grain and general merchandise, about 20,000 head of cattle and thousands of sheep were exported in 1895 by means of the Chesapeake & Ohio system.

The growth and success of the Chesapeake & Ohio's export business is due not alone to the traffic department, which secures the freight, but also to the transportation department, which moves it. The latter department is presided over by General Manager Stevens and Superintendent Doyle, who see to it that all traffic is handled with the greatest despatch possible.

At this point the interests of the company are well represented by Terminal Superintendent H. E. Parker, whose executive ability and fine qualifications fit him for the important position he occupies.

Captain W. N. Cooksey, the superintendent of floating property, is an official thoroughly familiar with all that pertains to his department, having a practical knowledge of ships and the sea.

Mr. J. W. Elliott, the general freight agent, is also well equipped for the responsibilities of his office. He has been with the company a long time and is one of its most valued agents.

These gentlemen are assisted by an able corps of assistants. In fact the interests of the Chesapeake & Ohio at this port are in capable hands, and for this reason it may be expected that the year 1896 will witness a development in the company's business here that was not dreamed of a few years ago.

Furness, Withy & Co., Limited, of which Sir Christopher Furness, M. P., is president, are the agents of the Chesapeake & Ohio Steamship Company. In addition to the six regular boats of this line, Furness, Withy & Co. have put on steamers for London, Liverpool, Glasgow, Dublin, Belfast and Rotterdam. Among these additional vessels, which are run by the Furness Line proper, are the "South, Gwalia," "Urd," "Oregon," "Sarnia," "Durham City," "Lambert's Point," "Ardrishaig," "Falls of Bracklin," and "Marie." Mr. A. E. Berner is the agent at this port for Furness, Withy & Co., and their interests could not be in more trustworthy or efficient hands.

**IN CONGRESS YESTERDAY.**

**Speaker Reed Has Signed the Bill to Accept the Ram Katahdin.**

[BY TELEGRAPH]

WASHINGTON, Jan. 3.—During the routine business of the morning hour, Mr. Morrill, chairman of the finance committee, moved that when the Senate adjourned today it be to meet on Tuesday next. He expressed the hope that at that time the finance committee would be able to report both the bond and tariff bills of the House. The motion was agreed to.

Mr. Hoar introduced, by request, a joint resolution proposing an amendment to the constitution of the United States so as to give the right of suffrage to women. He said that while he was in favor of the right of suffrage in women, he had supposed that it was hardly worth while for Congress [illegible] to the States until a larger number of States had adopted it for themselves, as they had a right to do. Referred to the judiciary committee.

Mr. George introduced a bill, for which unanimous consent was asked, to repeal the law which requires proof of loyalty during the war as a pre-requisite in any application for bounty land warrants to soldiers in the Mexican war.

The resolution offered by Mr. Sherman last Tuesday in relation to the reserve fund was laid before the Senate, and Mr. Sherman proceeded to address the Senate.

Senator Vest gave notice that he desired to speak upon the Sherman resolution next week and asked that it lie on the table. So ordered.

The resolution of Senator Elkins declaring it to be the sense of the Senate that hereafter no bonds be sold at private sale or under private contract was taken up, and Senator Elkins spoke in favor of it.

HOUSE OF REPRESENTATIVES.

The House reassembled today, under an arrangement heretofore announced by Mr. Dingley, merely for the purpose of adjourning until next Monday.

Speaker Reed announced that he had signed the bill to accept the ram Katahdin, and then at 12:05 the House adjourned.

**A Terrible Tragedy.**

BY TELEGRAPH.

MILLINGEVILLE, KY., Jan. 3.—A boy named Walters today shot two cousins, little girls, aged four and eight, and then sent a bullet into his own head. All three are fatally injured.

**Little Miss Chandler Entertains.**

[Written for the Daily Press.]

Miss Anne Boyd Chandler gave an "at home" from 7:00 to 9:00 on the night of New Year's, at the residence of her parents on Thirtieth street.

The spacious parlor was tastefully decorated with holly, cedar and mistletoe; and illuminated by dainty wax tapers, shedding soft light through pink shades.

After playing various games the young folks were invited to repair to the dining room, where there awaited them a table laden with a sumptuous collation of all the "goodies" their little hearts could wish for.

The winsome little hostess presided during the evening in her fascinating manner, and gave each one present a most delightful evening.

Among those present were Misses Louise Brumley, Jessie Shepherd, Nannie Turner, Marion Wilson and Mary Putzel, and Masters Charlie Brumley, George Benson, Charlie Epps, Frazer Bailey, Dick Davis, Bob Davis, and last but not least, the hostess of the evening.

# BUSINESS OF THE YEAR.

## Number of Failures Greater in 1895 Than in 1894.

## A COMPLICATED SITUATION.

**Railroad Earnings Show a Decided Improvement. Increase in Exports Warrant the Hope of a More Favorable Trade Balance.**

[BY TELEGRAPH.]

NEW YORK, Jan. 3.—Dun's Review places the number of commercial failures for 1895 at 13,197, against 8,085 for the previous year. The aggregate liabilities are slightly greater, though railroad earnings show a decided improvement.

Recently there has been a decrease in the imports of merchandise. Some increase in exports warrant the hope that the trade balance may be more favorable hereafter.

Rarely has there been a situation so complicated. Anything in the near future is difficult to forecast, but the impression is prevalent that a large sale of bonds will speedily revive confidence.

**CHILDREN'S HOME BURNED.**

**All the Inmates Saved. Fire Caused by a Gas Jet.**

[BY TELEGRAPH.]

COLUMBUS, O., Jan. 3.—The Franklin County Children's Home was burned early this morning. The 147 children in the home were just rising. The attendants hurriedly marched them from the building, and they were saved. A curtain blew against a gas jet and thus started the fire.

**TELEGRAPHIC BRIEFS.**

**Some of the Happenings of the World Concisely Told by Wire.**

WASHINGTON, Jan. 3.—Judge Peckham, who was recently appointed to the Supreme Court, will take the oath of office Monday.

BERLIN, Jan. 3.—The Emperor of Germany cabled congratulations today to the President of the South African Republic.

PHILADELPHIA, Jan. 3.—The strike of the motormen and conductors of the Union Traction Company went into nominal effect at 4 o'clock this [illegible] of 6,000 [illegible] are on strike.

WASHINGTON, Jan. 3.—There was an impression among some of the leading Republicans of the House today that the revenue bill, which was sent to the Senate last week, may pass that body.

**Special Sunday Trips.**

On Sunday, January 5, 1896, special trips will be made by the steamers of the Bay Line leaving terminal points on regular weekday schedule time and stopping at all regular landings.

Tickets, at the extremely low rate of $3 for the round trip, will be on sale at all offices Saturday, January 4, limited to 48 hours only. The steamer Alabama will leave Baltimore Sunday at 6:30 p. m. The steamer Georgia will leave Norfolk Sunday at the same time.

**Captured by Constable Madison.**

Special Constable E. C. Madison brought to this city yesterday a negro named James H. Holden, who burglarized the residence of Mr. L. H. Sargent at Lee Hall a few nights ago. The culprit was caught by Constable Madison in Williamsburg Thursday. He was given a hearing by Justice H. K. Harwood, of Lee Hall, who sent him on to the grand jury. He is now in jail awaiting indictment.

**Declining Our Pronouns.**

In a collection of the possessions of the late Robert Louis Stevenson there is a letter showing the difficulties which even such a master of English as he experienced in writing our language. "When I invent a language," he writes, "there shall be a direct and indirect pronoun differently declined, and then writing will be some fun." This idea he illustrates as follows:

Direct—He, him, his.
Indirect—Tu, tum, tus.

He adds in exemplification, "He seized tum by tus throat, but tu at the same moment caught him by his hair." A fellow would write hurricanes with an inflection like that.—Boston Herald.

**At the Restaurant.**

Guest—Why don't you smash those dishes?

Waitress—They fine us for smashing dishes here.

Guest—Well, if I ran the place, I'd fine you for not smashing them.—Detroit Free Press.

**Wasted Energy and Expense.**

A new advertising wagon introduced in New York is fitted up with two cylinders which keep revolving, giving a momentary view of various business announcements. There are people who would rather spend $10 to catch the eye of 2,000 or 3,000 people with a contraption of this kind than invest 50 cents to reach 100,000 readers in a good newspaper.—St. Louis Globe-Democrat.

Captain Crowley strikes a dapper pose around 1896 on the deck of an unidentified schooner. Tied up at the Chesapeake and Ohio pier, the ship is loaded with stacks of cord wood.

*Courtesy of Mariners Museum*

A newspaper advertisement in 1899 for the North Newport News Stage. The so-called North-End was then being developed.

*Courtesy of Newport News Public Library System*

The saying "dancing in the streets" included a bear in 1899. This dancing bear drew quite a crowd of Newport News residents, but the handler seems a little hesitant about his partner. West Avenue houses are in the background.

*Courtesy of Mariners Museum*

Looking east from the corner of King and Queen streets in Hampton before 1900 provides a good view of the city's streets. Before they were paved, large stones were spaced down the streets so ladies could walk downtown on the frequently muddy thoroughfares without ruining their garments.

Hampton was lively even then. There were plenty of bars for the thirsty and race tracks and harness racing for sporting enthusiasts.

*Courtesy of U.S. Army*

Endview Plantation has been a historical treasure since George Washington and his troops stopped there for water while marching to Yorktown. Built in 1781, in 1899 the home was visited by the wife of a Union soldier (far right) whose husband was cared for during the Civil War by the family of Dr. H.H. Curtis. The women with the soldier's wife are Maria Curtis (left) and Mrs. Curtis Taylor. The boys on the porch are Tom Shield (from left), Mingo Parker and Coleman Curtis. The identities of the women far left are unknown.

Wounded Union soldiers from the fight at Dam Number One were carried to the house, where they were cared for.

*Courtesy of Mrs. R.A. Clarke*

C. & O. R.R.
THE F. F. V. OF THE C. & O

Chesapeake and Ohio's "Fast Flying Virginian," dramatically portrayed by an artist, pulled orange coaches on its runs. The "Virginian" was one of the trains that ran from Newport News to Richmond just after the turn of the century.

*Courtesy of The Daily Press, Inc.*

Turn of the century fashions are illustrated by this family posing beside the river at Newport News in 1900.

*Courtesy of Mariners Museum*

In May 1900 repair work was completed on the bow of the four-masted steel bark *Dunstaffnage*. After the repairs were

An oxcart provides slow but sure transportation in 1900. One advantage this Lower Peninsula driver has over modern counterparts is that he doesn't have to worry about oil embargoes and the rising cost of gasoline.

*Courtesy of Mariners Museum*

completed at Newport News Shipbuilding, the *Dunstaffnage* waited at dockside.

*Courtesy of Newport News Shipbuilding*

In June 1900, Dry Dock 2 was under construction. The bottom of the excavation was about thirty-six feet below mean high water on the James River.

The foreground shows excavation at the entrance of the dock nearing completion while piling and timber work were progressing. The removal of earth and the handling of construction materials was done by means of trolleys suspended across the dock.

The background shows timber work and concrete bottom at the head of the dock complete. The caisson gate for the dock was being built there and, upon completion and flooding of the dock, was to be floated to its place across the entrance.

*Courtesy of Newport News Shipbuilding*

When Newport News Shipbuilding dry docked two large schooners simultaneously, they were docked stern to stern with the bowsprits overreaching the ends of the dock. In September 1900, the five-master *Nathaniel T. Palmer* (rear) and four-master *Mary E. Palmer* were docked in such fashion.

# THE LATE HARRISON PHOEBUS,

## HIS LIFE AND DEATH.

Came an angel in the morning,
When the tide went out to sea,
Saying there is one among you
That must rise and go with me.
To the sound of lamentation,
Muffled drum and cannon's roll,
From the site of old Fort Monroe,
Passed a brave man's soul.

To the starry cluster beaming,
In the blue of midnight skies,
Ancients say a star is added,
When a good man dies:
And amid the evening ether,
When the guns of sunset roll
O'er the site of old Fort Monroe,
Shines a good man's soul.

M. T.

The community was shocked on Thursday morning to hear that the relentless hand of death had been laid upon one whom it least expected, and whom it could least spare. Mr. Harrison Phoebus, the proprietor of the Hygeia Hotel, is no more. But a few days ago in health and strength, with prospects of a long life and a useful and prosperous one, he was suddenly stricken with disease, and on Thursday morning at six o'clock, his spirit passed to God who gave it.

Mr. Phœbus's life and early struggles have been portrayed in most of the leading journals of the day, until many persons all over the country are better acquainted with it that with that of many of our public men

Born in Somerset County, Md., near Princess Anne, in 1840, of poor but respectable, hard-working parents, his early life was that of a poor country lad. He was the youngest of sixteen children. His father died before he had entered his teens, leaving his mother with a large family to support. He worked hard to aid his widowed parent in her great task, and therefore had little opportunity to acquire any education, except what he could secure at a district school during an often interrupted attendance of a few winters. All that he could earn went into the family treasury, and up to his eighteenth year he knew not what it was to spend a dollar for himself. But as he was ambitious, and as he approached his majority, he devoted all of his leisure hours to reading and satisfying a natural taste he had for mechanics.

When but 15 years of age he worked hard at tonging oysters for which he received 50 cents a day, the whole of which was cheerfully and conscientiously carried home to his mother.

He taught himself the use of tools, and, from a stray copy of Pitman's Phonography, he learned short hand writing. At 18 he was a contractor for saw-mill hauling; at 19 he was a master-builder in a small way; at 21 he enlisted in a Maryland Federal regiment and was honorably discharged in 1863.

HARRISON PHOEBUS.

He was in Baltimore, without money, but full of vigor, and was seeking work where he could master circumstances and make opportunities. Chance led him to the Adams Express office, where he saw a great deal of work going on in an orderly and systematic manner.

"Who hires the men here?" he asked of a gentleman standing by.

"I do," was the reply. "What do you want?"

"Work," replied young Phoebus.

"What can you do?"

"I can sweep the floor, I can load a wagon, or I can write a letter."

He was hired as a wagoner at $3 a week. In 10 days he was at work in the office. In six weeks he was detailed as a special messenger on the way train to Martinsburg, W. Va. He did other important and responsible work for the company until 1866, when he was appointed its agent at Fortress Monroe. Mr Samuel M. Shoemaker, the Baltimore manager of the express company, had learned Mr Phoebus' worth and was his fast friend. Besides his work as express agent at Fortress Monroe, he became postmaster, was agent for several transportation lines, built up a large insurance business, and was a notary public and United States commissioner. He made profitable investments in real estate, and with his industry, ability and integrity, made successful everything he handled.

In 1872 the old Hygeia Hotel, which had been a great resort before the war, and had been torn down during its continuance, was rebuilt. The proprietors, however, did not make a success of it, and, for two years, it had a mercurial existence, until Mr. Phoebus, recognizing the field as a promising one, purchased the structure, in 1874, still retaining his interest in all other businesses. Since then the history of the hotel has been one of brilliant success. It quickly grew in reputation through the methods of its popular proprietor, until it has frequently been unable to accomodate the hundreds and thousands that flocked to its health-promising apartments. As his patrons increased, so has Mr. Phoebus improved his hostelry, until now it has no superior and few equals in the country in size, comfort and all appurtenances of the trade. It is indeed a grand monument to the unflagging energy, severe, hard work and strict self-discipline of Mr. Phoebus.

As to the private character and life of Mr. Phoebus, it is almost as well known as his public. A kind husband, an indulgent father and a firm, staunch friend. His hand was always open to aid the poor and needy, but in his giving he was unostentatious. While burdened with the management of his immense private business, yet his ear was always open and his advice always ready to anyone in business difficulty; and if he was satisfied of the ability and push of the party, more substantial aid was always forthcoming.

Those who have visited the Point periodically will now miss the genial smile, the warm grasp of the hand, and the kindly interest of its former proprietor, but his memory will be warm in the hearts of those who knew him intimately long after the earthly casket which held his noble spirit has mouldered into dust.

Mrs. Phoebus has the undivided sympathy of all classes in this her sudden and sad bereavement, and it is hoped she may have strength given her to bear up under the burden thus laid upon her. Fortunate is she to have the support of her noble sons, upon the shoulders of each of whom may the mantle of their father fall.

On Thursday an autopsy was held by the undersigned physicians, who reudered the followiug certificate.

*February 25th, 1886.*

We, the undersigned physicians, having this day made an autopsy on the cadaver of Harrison Phoebus, who, when alive, was personally known to each of us, do hereby certify, to the best of our knowledge and belief, that the death of the said Harrison Phoebus which occurred at about 6 a. m., of this date, was caused by a rupture of the right auricle of the heart, and the effusion of blood into the pericardium, and that the said rupture of the wall of the said auricle was due to fatty degeneration of the tissues thereof.

CHAS. SELDEN, M. D.
J. A. BAILEY, SURG., U. S. A.
S. K. TOWLE, " N. M. H.
—— TORNEY, ASST. SURG., U. S. A.

Mill Creek was a sleepy little village outside Fort Monroe when the Civil War broke out, but the war brought an overflow of troops to Camp Hamilton outside Fort Monroe. The town was enlarged, and the name changed to Chesapeake City.

After Harrison Phoebus came to Fort Monroe to manage the Hygeia Hotel, his efforts resulted in the Chesapeake and Ohio Railway being extended into Chesapeake City. The town was renamed Phoebus in his honor when it was incorporated as a town in 1900. It was consolidated with the City of Hampton in July 1952. Easily accessible to soldiers from Fort Monroe, the town has experienced periodic booms and declines.

*Courtesy of Syms-Eaton Museum*

On a crisp October afternoon in 1901, the Pacific Mail liner *Siberia* was launched at Newport News Shipbuilding. It was a special occasion at Newport News because the launching occurred on the 120th anniversary of the surrender of Cornwallis at Yorktown, and it was the twentieth anniversary of the centennial observance at Yorktown, which had celebrated the beginning of railroad service to Newport News.

*Courtesy of Newport News Shipbuilding*

At the time of its incorporation in 1900, Phoebus had more than 2,000 inhabitants. The city consisted of a wooden school house, a volunteer fire department, some grocery and general stores, plenty of saloons, a bank, and hotels, one of which was Fuller's Hotel, at Mallory and County Streets, depicted in this 1903 photograph.

*Courtesy of The Daily Press, Inc.*

SYMS-EATON ACADEMY

Scheduled for destruction in late 1976 or 1977 to make way for redevelopment in Hampton, the Syms-Eaton Academy building is a reminder of the first free schools in the United States.

The schools provided for in the wills of Benjamin Syms and Thomas Eaton were officially consolidated in 1805 as Hampton Academy.

After the original property was sold, Hampton Academy was built on Cary Street but was burned in the Civil War.

The Syms-Eaton Academy was built in 1902 near the site of Hampton Academy and was the only elementary school in Hampton from 1902 until 1930.

The building currently serves as headquarters for the Hampton School Board and administration.

*Photo by Bea Kopp*

Billy Sunday, who played baseball with the Chicago White Stockings, Pittsburgh Pittsburgs and Philadelphia Phillies, left sports to become a minister in 1903. With strong promotion and a flamboyant style, he became the era's most popular evangelist.

Said to have converted more than a million people to Christianity, he undoubtedly won a few Peninsula souls during his sermons in April 1925. His tabernacle, a temporary wooden building, was located on the Casino Grounds in Newport News.

*Courtesy of The Daily Press, Inc.*

The Silsby Building, from an old postcard, was also known as the Law Building because it housed many of Newport News' attorneys.

It had an even more unique feature, however. A metal time ball, which was cloth-covered, was dropped at noon daily from the pole on the top of the building at the right of the spire.

Seamen set their clocks according to the ball until the device was dismantled in the 1950's.

Located on 27th Street and Washington Avenue, the building dates back to 1904. It was compared to the Leaning Tower of Pisa because it began to lean away from the building adjacent to it. It was torn down in 1963.

*Courtesy of H. Reid*

A view of Newport News Shipbuilding in September 1906 that may well be unique in the annals of American sailing vessels -- five schooners of three, four, five, six (partially visible), and the world's only seven master. The ships are:

Three masts -- *Salie I'On*
Four masts -- *Malcolm Baxter, Jr.*
Five masts -- Unknown
Six masts -- *Eleanor A. Percy*
Seven masts -- *Thomas W. Lawson*

*Courtesy of Newport News Shipbuilding*

Hampton Fire Department was ready to roll about 1907. Located on Court Street, the fire department occupied the present site of the city treasurer's office. Founded in 1884, the department was begun to meet a need clearly established by a devastating fire that struck the city that year. The fire destroyed more than thirty buildings.

*Courtesy of Billy Teagle*

five-masted schooner lying off Newport
ews in 1907 was probably photographed by
e late Charles C. Epes.

*Courtesy of Mariners Museum*

A postcard provides a look at 28th Street in Newport News in the early 1900's. Buxton and Parker (building on right) was one of the city's finest furnishings stores.

*Courtesy of Newport News Public Library System*

When a whale washed up on Buckroe Beach in 1909, it quickly drew a crowd of curious spectators.

*Courtesy of Newport News Public Library System*

Before the clatter of hooves was replaced by the sound of screeching brakes in Newport News, Conard's Horse Shoeing Shop did a steady business. Located on Huntington Avenue, the shop is about to work on two customers in 1910.

*Courtesy of Mariners Museum*

A funeral procession honors men killed in a gun explosion at Fort Monroe on July 21, 1910.

A firing exercise was scheduled the day of the accident, but the occasion, attended by notables and curious onlookers, turned to tragedy when one of the guns on DeRussy Battery exploded during the exercise. Eleven men were killed.

*Courtesy of U.S. Army*

What a way to travel. This was the plush interior of the special parlorcar of the Newport News and Hampton Railway Gas and Electric Co., formed by a merger of existing companies in 1914. The private vehicle was used by President John N. Shanahan and also was available for hire. It was furnished with padded wicker chairs, carpeting and curtains. The elegant car met VIPs at the steamboat dock at Old Point Comfort and the C & O depot.

*Courtesy of The Daily Press, Inc.*

Before the United States entered World War I, the German commerce raider *Kronprinz Wilhelm,* formerly a crack passenger liner, anchored off Newport News in April 1915. The cruiser evaded a blockading British cruiser to seek sanctuary in a neutral port.

Built in 1901, the coal-burner had an admirable record as a commerce raider. She captured or destroyed more than a dozen ships before coming to Newport News. She sank some of her victims by ramming, and the warfare had taken its toll on both the vessel and men.

After Newport News Shipbuilding did some essential repair work, she was interned along with the *Prinz Eitel Friedrich,* another German commerce raider which also had escaped the British. Both were taken to the Portsmouth Navy Yard. When America entered the war, the crewmen became prisoners of war, and the ship was taken over by the U.S. Navy. The *Kronprinz Wilhelm* became the *USS Von Steuben,* a troop transport. The *Prinz Eitel Friedrich* became another transport, the *USS Dekalb.*

*Courtesy of Mariners Museum*

Curtiss Flying School provided training for some of the country's greatest aviators, including General Billy Mitchell, during its existence from 1915 to 1922. Located by the Newport News-Sewells Point ferry slip, the school was headed by Captain Thomas Baldwin. Many of the men who trained in planes such as these went on to serve in the famous Lafayette Escadrille.

*Courtesy of H. Reid*

Former President William H. Taft paid a visit to Newport News Shipbuilding in April 1917. Taft spoke to a large crowd of workers about preparedness for war. The topic was a timely one, coming three weeks after a declaration of war by the United States.

*Courtesy of Newport News Shipbuilding*

Phoebus looks dead, particularly around the Palace Hotel, in February 1918. But business picked up in the early 1920's when soldiers and sailors from the military bases poured into the town. Those years also brought fishing trawlers into port as the seafood industry boomed.

*Courtesy of The Daily Press, Inc.*

In the latter part of 1916 it became apparent that housing under construction in Newport News would be inadequate for the growing labor force at Newport News Shipbuilding. In the spring of 1917 the company began building houses for sale to employees. These homes, looking up Virginia Avenue from 46th Street, were completed and occupied in April 1918.

*Courtesy of Newport News Shipbuilding*

# HILTON VILLAGE

Hilton Village was part of the Shipping Board's war program for providing accommodations when congestion of Newport News prevented needed increases in the yard force for repairing vessels and building new ships. Newport News Shipbuilding commenced preliminary planning for the purchase and development of a site in January 1918, pending the organization of a more suitable means for carrying out the work. A separate company was formed under a real estate charter to manage the project.

At that time all open space immediately north of Newport News was occupied or reserved for use by Army camps. The site selected, about three miles north of the shipyard, was covered with a thick growth of trees.

After the Shipbuilding Realty Corporation was organized by officers of Newport News Shipbuilding, and upon approval of plans and authorization of construction by the Shipping Board, the clearing of the site was begun in April 1918.

At the time of the Armistice in November, 138 houses had been completed and occupied, with fifty-eight more nearly ready for occupancy. The project, originally designed for 500 families, was thereafter curtailed to 473.

The village was sold in 1922 to private interests, and the houses were made available to individual purchasers; the village became a home-owning community.

This series of pictures follows the story of Hilton Village, which has been recognized by the Historic Landmark Commission, from the original clearing of the land to the 1970's.

The original clearing was done the hard way -- with mules.

*Courtesy of Newport News Public Library System*

C

This is Warwick?

*Courtesy of Newport News Public Library System*

Things are beginning to take shape.

*Courtesy of Newport News Public Library System*

Hilton's architectural style makes it unique.

*Courtesy of Newport News Public Library System*

A view up Warwick Boulevard in 1975.

*Photo by Bea Kopp*

This photograph of Hampton, looking west down Queen Street in 1918, may well have been taken during the Spanish influenza epidemic that terrorized residents. The epidemic reached its peak in October. Thirty people died of pneumonia in Hampton and Phoebus during the month, and 71 of the influenza.

The problem was so serious that the governor banned public gatherings throughout the state. Although the quarantine was lifted at the end of October, people continued to die, but in lesser numbers. More than 11,000 Virginians died of the dreaded disease.

*Courtesy of U.S. Army*

These soldiers from Camp Stuart were part of the teeming mass of soldiers and workers who came together in the war effort. After the war, Camp Stuart served as a training base for merchant seamen before it was destroyed. Ultimately, Stuart Gardens, a residential section, came to occupy the site.

*Courtesy of The Daily Press, Inc.*

These balloonists were a familiar site at Camp Eustis in 1918. They were part of the 20th, 26th and 42nd balloon companies training at Lee Hall Balloon School on the post.

The aerialists performed admirably in France after their training. Perched in wicker baskets, which hung from hydrogen-filled balloons made of scraps of rubber-coated canvas that were sewn and glued together, the balloonists were in constant danger from German planes.

They were easy targets, but were able to parachute to safety when German pilots cut short their reconnaissance.

*Courtesy of U.S. Army*

Thousands of American troops returned from Europe to Newport News after World War I. These Ohio artillery troops came marching home March 24, 1919. This view is looking west on 25th Street, soon redesignated Victory Avenue.

*Courtesy of Newport News Public Library System*

Returning soldiers were a familiar sight in Newport News at the end of World War I. Young men returned from Europe and were greeted by the Victory Arch dedicated April 13, 1919. The original wood and plaster arch was constructed to honor the men who fought in the war and as a memorial to those who died. It proved impossible to maintain, however, so a more sturdy duplicate was dedicated on May 30, 1962.

*Courtesy of Bea Kopp*

Welcome home ceremonies would have to go a long way to top festivities on May 20, 1919, when Virginia soldiers of the 29th Division returned from France. The crowd is gathering on Washington Avenue near 25th and 26th Streets in Newport News to pay tribute to the returning heroes.

*Courtesy of The Daily Press, Inc.*

Today, when the noon meal is frequently a cheeseburger and an order of fries, this lunchtime scene at Newport News Shipbuilding in 1919 seems rather strange. Note the ice cream wagon among the caterers.

*Courtesy of Mariners Museum*

The Casino grounds and 25th Street were almost deserted in this circa 1920 photograph. At lower right is the rear of the post office. The building at top left was a temporary structure built during World War I.

*Courtesy of Bea Kopp*

# LANGLEY FIELD

Although it's difficult to believe, wooden hangars constituted Langley Field's flight line around 1919.

Even though the land for the field was bought by the government in 1916, Langley Field wasn't named until August 1917.

Named for Samuel P. Langley, an aviation pioneer, the field was used jointly by the Army Air Corps and the National Advisory Committee for Aeronautics. The first military members arrived in 1917. Construction was still underway when at the end of the year 38 officers and 409 enlisted men were stationed there.

In the early days there was an aerial photography school, aerial observer school and a site for testing "Jennys." In March 1919, two balloon companies were added to the field.

Langley Field also was an important element in General Billy Mitchell's efforts to prove the value of aircraft against naval vessels; his First Provisional Air Brigade trained at Langley in 1921. Mitchell, who learned to fly at the Curtiss Flying School in Newport News, later directed a bombing test that sank three former German ships used as target vessels. His point was made.

A large number of lighter-than-air craft also was stationed at the field; the most famous was the *Roma*, which crashed in February 1922.

Over the years, additional land has been added to the base, particularly in 1934 and 1941, when expansion was necessary to meet military needs during the war. During World War II, Langley was an important training center for military personnel. Following the war, the base was selected as permanent home of Tactical Air Command.

In 1958, the National Advisory Committee for Aeronautics became the National Aeronautics and Space Administration. NASA's Langley Research Center has received worldwide recognition for its contributions to the country's space program.

*Courtesy of U.S. Air Force*

One of Langley Air Force Base's most illustrious visitors over the years was Orville Wright in July 1922. Wright was a member of NACA's advisory committee.

*Courtesy of U.S. Air Force*

The tragic story of the U.S. Army airship *Roma* began when the 410-foot dirigible was purchased from Italy in 1921 and shipped to Langley Field. The lighter-than-air ship performed fairly well on three test flights, but on the fourth flight from Langley Field, February 21, 1922, the test ended in tragedy.

Malfunctioning equipment caused the *Roma* to lose altitude over the Norfolk Army Base. After hitting high voltage lines, the ship burst into flames, fueled by its hydrogen and gasoline in the fuel tanks.

Only eleven men survived the crash out of the 45-man crew. The victims' bodies were charred almost beyond recognition. On February 24, the dead men were honored by a public funeral held on Newport News' Casino grounds near the Victory Arch. These photographs show the *Roma* about to take off on the ill-fated voyage and the funeral procession for the victims entering the grounds by way of 26th Street.

*Courtesy of Syms-Eaton Museum*

Peninsula school children put on their own patriotic display in 1925. The children, marching to the beat of a drum which is partially obscured by a telephone pole, are dressed in what appear to be homemade hats as they parade down the street with their flags.

*Courtesy of Mariners Museum*

These before and after views of the *SS Leviathan* are two of the most important photographs in Newport News history.

The "naval holiday" after World War I was no holiday for the city's residents. Naval contracts with Newport News Shipbuilding worth millions of dollars were cancelled, and in 1922, the city was on the brink of disaster.

When the U.S. Shipping Board requested bids on the reconversion of the *SS Leviathan*, a German passenger liner that had been converted into a U.S. troop ship during the war, Newport News Shipbuilding president

Homer L. Ferguson was determined to win the contract.

And he did. His bid, intentionally below cost, was $2 million below its nearest competitor, and the *SS Leviathan* came to Newport News, welcomed as the savior she was.

Work on the vessel, which was the world's largest at the time, provided jobs for about 2,500 employees. When the *SS Leviathan* left Newport News in 1923, the parting was sad because it might well be said that she had kept Newport News Shipbuilding and the town alive.

*Courtesy of Newport News Shipbuilding*

Washington Avenue was the primary business artery in Newport News in the early 1920's. This view is looking north from 25th Street. The Silsby Building is in the background right.

*Courtesy of Bea Kopp*

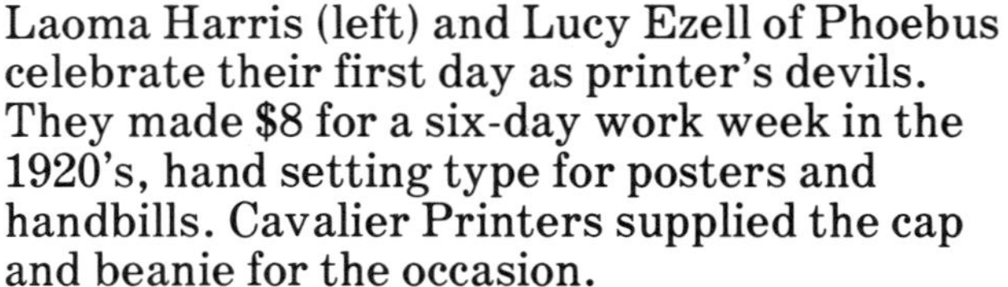

Laoma Harris (left) and Lucy Ezell of Phoebus celebrate their first day as printer's devils. They made $8 for a six-day work week in the 1920's, hand setting type for posters and handbills. Cavalier Printers supplied the cap and beanie for the occasion.

*Courtesy of Lucy Ezell*

Langley received an important visitor in 1928. Amelia Earhart, who was a liberated woman long before the idea really caught on, poses with Dr. Henry J.E. Reid (to her left) of NACA and Lieutenant Colonel W.S. Wuest, base commander (far right).

*Courtesy of U.S. Air Force*

# FORT EUSTIS

Mulberry Island was mostly rural in 1918 when construction was begun on Camp Eustis, named for General Abraham Eustis. The Coast Artillery Training School, located at Fort Monroe, needed more firing space for training, so land for Camp Eustis was purchased, and nearly 40,000 workers helped build the original camp.

Artillery training continued after the war, and the name was changed to Fort Eustis in 1922. But two years after the 1929 stock market crash, the post was abandoned owing to a cutback in military expenditures. The facility then became a correction camp for delinquents and a Works Progress Administration camp.

When military needs again came to the fore in 1940, Fort Eustis was reactivated, becoming the Coast Artillery Training Center with emphasis on anti-aircraft artillery. The war also brought a substantial need for Transportation Corps officers, and the Army's Transportation School came into existence. As demands increased, the school was moved to different locations, but centralization of the various elements was needed.

In May 1946, Transportation School was located at Fort Eustis because the site had a deep water harbor, beaches, channels inland and plenty of land.

In 1950, the Transportation Corps became a permanent branch of the Army, and over the years, Fort Eustis-trained solders have proved their worth from the icy Alaskan landscape to the jungles of Vietnam.

Fort Eustis soldiers prove that the Army life sometimes can be a picnic. Members of the mechanized forces are having a quick lunch in January 1930. Eating while on the march was possible because of gasoline-fueled kitchens mounted on trucks.

*Courtesy of U.S. Army*

The cruiser *Houston* was in Newport News Shipbuilding's Dry Dock 2 being fitted out in March 1930. The *USS Houston* was sunk in 1942 by Japanese vessels. She went down with her ensign still flying, and she was awarded the Presidential Unit Citation.

*Courtesy of Newport News Shipbuilding*

# HAMPTON INSTITUTE

Students coming out of Hampton Institute's Robert Ogden Auditorium about 1930 look a bit different from today's college students.

The college was founded by Samuel Chapman Armstrong, a Union general, shortly after the Civil War.

Armstrong was sent to Hampton by the Freedmen's Bureau to help the thousands of former slaves who took refuge on the Peninsula.

Impressed by the black soldiers who had served under him during the war, Armstrong's dream was to establish a normal school to teach blacks to teach each other.

Armstrong, the son of missionary parents in Hawaii, enlisted the aid of the American Missionary Association and opened Hampton Normal and Agricultural Institute in April 1868 with two teachers and fifteen students. Studies were directed toward "Education for Life."

Classes were held in a converted farmhouse and barracks until the first structure, the Academy Building, was completed. When weather was pleasant, classes were held in the shade of the giant Emancipation Oak, where the Emancipation Proclamation was read to Hampton residents in 1863.

For the first few years, there were no dormitories. Men lived in army tents, and women lived in barracks. Money for the first residence hall was raised through tours by the Hampton Singers, which continue to give concerts throught the United States and Europe.

In addition to pioneering in higher education for blacks, the institute was a leader in Indian education. After Indian hostilities ended in 1875, seventy-five Indian leaders were taken as prisoners to serve as examples and brought East by the Government. After three years as prisoners, they were freed and offered free transportation back to their homes in the West. Some of the Indians, however, chose to remain in the East to further their educations. At midnight on April 18, 1878, fifteen of them, mostly Kiowas and Cheyennes, arrived to begin their studies.

Indians continued to come to Hampton Institute until after the turn of the century, and between 1878 and 1912, it served as a federally funded Indian base.

In 1922, the institute first offered courses leading to the bachelor of science degree, and ten years later the school earned full accreditation as a four-year college.

Today, Hampton Institute is a sprawling campus with numerous modern structures blending with the original buildings. Graduates such as Booker T. Washington, founder of Tuskegee Institute, have fulfilled Armstrong's dream of helping blacks reach their potential.

*Courtesy of The Daily Press, Inc.*

PHOEBUS FIRE DEPARTMENT
PHOEBUS COMPANY

The Phoebus Fire Department of modern times has come a long way from the 1930 version. The city's volunteer fire department got an early start when it was founded by residents in 1893, seven years before the town was incorporated; the initial company started out with about two hundred dollars.

*Courtesy of The Daily Press, Inc.*

Newsboys from the *Daily Press* strike a handsome pose in front of the old Buckroe Hotel in July, 1932. The *Daily Press* sponsored a yearly outing for its newsboys.

*Courtesy of The Daily Press, Inc.*

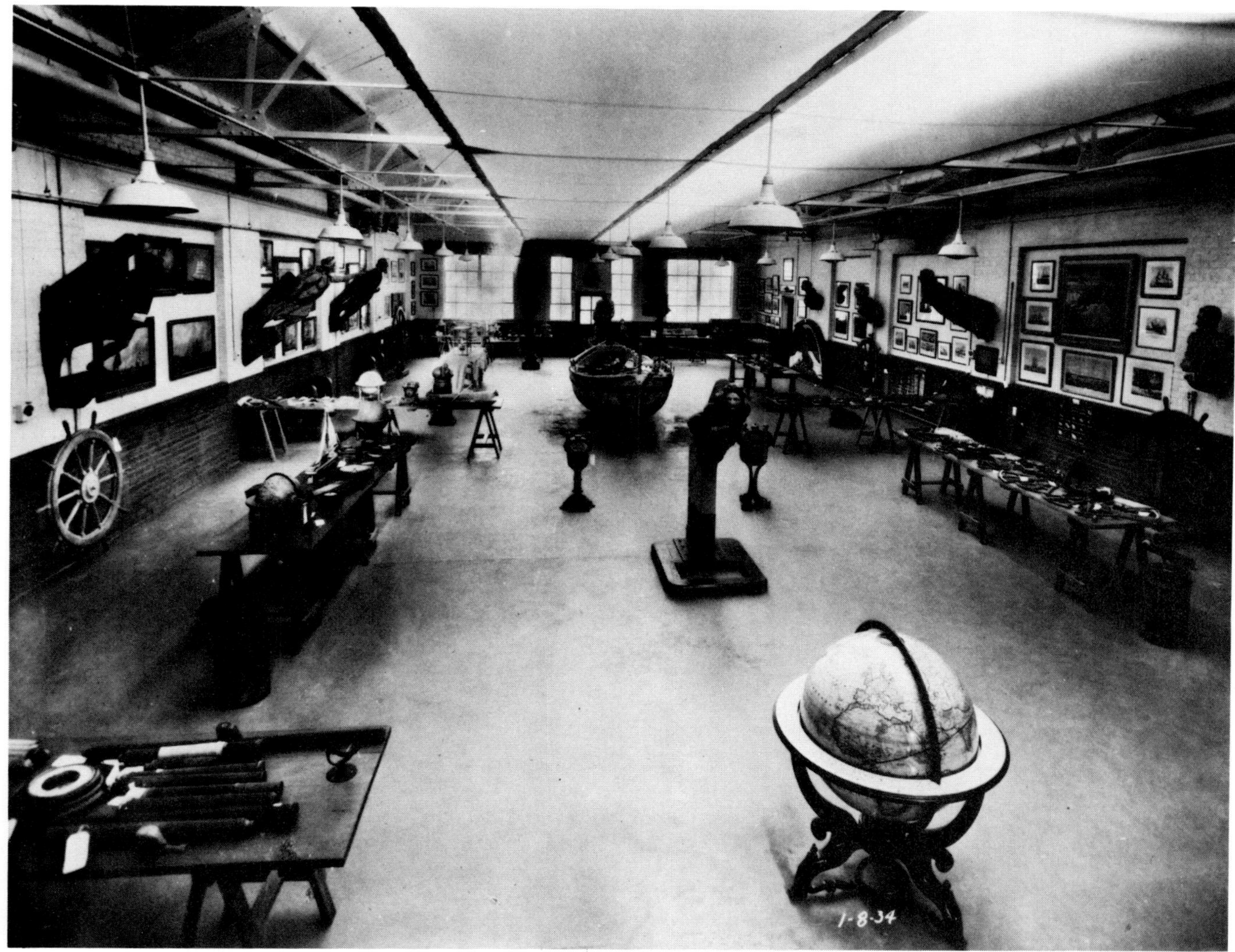


Founded by Archer M. Huntington, a principal owner of Newport News Shipbuilding, Mariners Museum in Newport News was opened to the public in October 1933.

This view of the original gallery in the museum illustrates the somewhat crude display methods compared to current exhibits. These objects are wired to sawhorse-type tables.

Today, the main building stands on grounds of more than 800 acres which include the museum, Lake Maury (named after the "Pathfinder of the Seas," Matthew Fontaine Maury) and park.

The museum is a treasure trove of nautical art objects, illustrations and small craft.

*Courtesy of Mariners Museum*

In June 1931, these Fort Eustis tanks probably seemed deadly while moving over rough terrain. Advances in military weapons make them seem almost like toys today.

*Courtesy of U.S. Army*

M. H. FISH

Peninsula oldtimers aren't exaggerating when they talk about the devastation of the 1933 flood. As this view of Hampton's Queen Street, August 23, 1933, points out, the canoe was as dependable a means of transportation as the automobile.

The hurricane and its repercussions resulted in three deaths on the Peninsula. Damages came to more than $3 million.

*Courtesy of The Daily Press, Inc.*

LANGLEY
SINS OF MAN
ALSO FINE SHORTS

The 14,500-ton *USS Ranger*, camouflaged and steaming at sea during World War II, was the first vessel designed and built from the keel up as an aircraft carrier. The carrier was commissioned in June 1934, more than a year after her launching at Newport News Shipbuilding. She was christened by Mrs. Herbert Hoover on February 25, 1933.

*Courtesy of U.S. Navy*

Langley Theater was playing *Sins of Man* and fine shorts in 1936. Wonder if there's a connection?

On Queen Street in Hampton, the well-known theater was torn down in March 1968. The theater closed its doors the previous year with a simple newspaper notice: "We are closed, will not reopen. Thank you for your patronage."

The closing ended almost fifty years of entertainment since the theater had opened as Scott Theater in 1920.

*Courtesy of Leslie Ange, Jr.*

Lieutenant General Frank M. Andrews, commanding general of General Headquarters, greets Major Barney M. Giles, pilot of the first Boeing B-17 to land at Langley Air Force Base, in March 1937.

*Courtesy of U.S. Air Force*

Construction workers dig in at the corner of East Mellon and South Willard streets in Phoebus in the 1930's.

*Courtesy of The Daily Press, Inc.*

Apprentice alumni are assembled at the Huntington Monument in August 1937. The first certificate of completion for the required four-year apprenticeship course was issued in April 1894. In 1895, about fifty apprentices were reported in the machine shop with lesser numbers employed in the joiner, pattern, boiler and copper shops and other departments.

*Courtesy of Newport News Shipbuilding*

On April 15, 1942, military prisoners at Fort Monroe buried twenty-nine German sailors from *U-85*, a submarine sunk by the *USS Roper*, a destroyer patrolling the North Carolina coast.

The U-boat was the first enemy submarine destroyed by a Navy ship in the war. For security reasons, the bodies were taken to Hampton National Cemetery under the strictest secrecy.

*Courtesy of U.S. Army*

This Buckroe Beach streetcar was near Hampton Institute in July 1940. Streetcars were a major means of transportation on the Peninsula until buses took over in 1946. On Saturday nights in the early 1900's, streetcars were filled with people heading for dances at the Chamberlin Hotel, and during the summer, at Buckroe Beach.

*Courtesy of Bea Kopp*

*Courtesy of Mariners Museum*

Newport News Shipbuilding had a full head of steam when the Japanese bombed Pearl Harbor in December 1941. The shipyard hummed with activity, and the city of Newport News, bursting at the seams, had more than 60,000 people. As in World War I, it was packed with workers and military personnel. The housing shortages and inconveniences were major.

The Hampton Roads Port of Embarkation, established during World War I, was reactivated in 1942; Camp Patrick Henry, carved out of Warwick County woods, was the staging area for thousands of troops who were to be shipped overseas, some of whom are depicted here .

Although the war placed difficult demands on the citizens, they rallied to meet them. Countless tons of supplies and more than one-and-a-half million military personnel passed through Newport News as a result of the war. The area's wartime accomplishments can be remembered with pride.

In September 1945, citizens greeted returning troops aboard the *USS General Le Roy Eltinge* with a band (right).

*Courtesy of The Daily Press, Inc.*

Regrettably, the identities of these third grade students at Woodrow Wilson Elementary School in Newport News are not known. It would be particularly interesting to know the identity of the young man (front right) who is gallantly bowing despite the fact that he has ripped the seat out of his pants. But after all, it was a May Day dance in the early 1940's, and even then, the show had to go on.

*Photo by Bea Kopp*

The *SS America* was nudged away from a Newport News Shipbuilding pier shortly after her reconversion to passenger service in 1946. Originally commissioned in 1940, the 33,000-ton *America* was the largest merchant ship ever built in the country when Eleanor Roosevelt smashed a bottle of champagne across her bow.

World War II brought the need for transports, so she was acquired by the government in 1942, converted to a troop transport and renamed the *USS West Point*.

The liner served ably during the war, but although she was able to evade German submarines, the vessel was not able to escape changing times. In 1964 the *SS America* was sold by the U.S. Lines and became the Greek passenger liner *Australis*.

*Photo by Bea Kopp*

July weather hasn't changed on the Peninsula over the years. In 1951, Buckroe Beach was packed with people anxious to cool off.

*Courtesy of The Daily Press, Inc.*

A view of Old Point Comfort in 1954 illustrates the famous moat. Completed in 1834, it became the location of the Army's first artillery school. After several changes and reorganizations, in 1973 the U.S. Army Training and Doctrine Command was established at the historical fort.

*Courtesy of U.S. Army*

Millions of cars have passed through the toll gates into the Hampton Roads Bridge Tunnel since it opened to traffic November 1, 1957. The $62 million project brought an end to ferry service established in 1819 between the Peninsula and Norfolk.

Perhaps, more than any other event, it signaled the beginning of a new era for the Peninsula. Construction is currently underway to provide two-lane traffic in each direction, as shown in this 1975 photograph.

*Photo by Jim Livengood*
*Courtesy of The Daily Press, Inc.*

Before completion, Hampton Roads Bridge Tunnel looked like a bomb shelter.

*Courtesy of The Daily Press, Inc.*

It's difficult to determine when this photograph was taken without even one car visible in the normally busy tunnel.

*Courtesy of The Daily Press, Inc.*

Tugs bring the *SS United States* into Newport News in December 1957 for her annual overhaul. The luxury liner, built at Newport News Shipbuilding in 1952, usually returned to the city every year for overhaul.

With a crew of 1,000, she set the world speed record for the Atlantic crossing in three days, ten hours and forty minutes on her maiden voyage in 1952.

*SS United States* carried such celebrities as Elizabeth Taylor and the Duke and Duchess of Windsor in her heydey, but today she's mothballed in Norfolk, the victim of changing times.

*Courtesy of Newport News Shipbuilding*

On a foggy January morning in 1957 "The Sportsman," westbound C & O train No. 47, pulled into Hampton Roads Transfer Station.

Although passenger service by rail largely has been supplanted by air travel, railroads continue to serve as a vital link in this country's shipping network.

*Photo by Alexander C. Brown*

One of the problems with growth is that old buildings tend to disappear in the process. Looking north down Washington Avenue in 1958 brings a good view of the Commercial Hotel -- a last look, however, because the hotel has been destroyed.

*Courtesy of The Daily Press, Inc.*

When the cities of Newport News and Warwick merged July 1, 1958, into the city of Newport News, the occasion was marked by a ribbon-cutting ceremony. Mrs. Phillip Hiden (left) and Mrs. Homer L. Ferguson were aided by J.B. Woodward, Jr. (carnation in coat), chairman of the board of Newport News Shipbuilding. The giant scissors used here were made for the opening of the James River Bridge in 1928.

*Photo by Bea Kopp*

The destruction of the U.S. Restaurant on 25th Street eliminated one of Newport News' most frequented night spots. The restaurant, far right in this 1958 photograph, was a hangout for newspaper reporters, musicians and traveling salesmen.

At one time it was the only all-night restaurant in the city, and it was especially known for its steaming coffee and interesting night people. Today the location is occupied by a city hall parking lot.

*Courtesy of Bea Kopp*

An aerial view from the Hotel Warwick looks down 25th Street in the 1960's. The first building on the right is the hotel's annex; Citizens Marine Jefferson Bank is mid-way down the street on the left and the downtown Sears is in the background left.

*Courtesy of The Daily Press, Inc.*

U.S. Grill

On March 6, 1962, heavy winds and snow signalled the beginning of a storm that would last until March 8 and cause millions of dollars of damage in Hampton and Newport News.

Known as the Ash Wednesday storm, the destruction was caused by abnormally high tides of a size seen only a few times a century, and winds gusting up to sixty miles per hour which pushed the water inland. The surging flood was particularly damaging to beachfront property, but miraculously there was no loss of life.

When the water finally receded, sand and debris littered the area as Peninsula residents began the arduous job of picking up the pieces.

This photograph shows the hard-hit Resort Boulevard at Buckroe Beach.

*Photo by Jim Livengood*
*Courtesy of The Daily Press, Inc.*

The surf sprays skyward at Fort Monroe's seawall during the Ash Wednesday storm.

*Courtesy of The Daily Press, Inc.*

Looking back on the flood's devastation, one is a bit more likely to see the humor implied by the name of River Street in Hampton.

*Photo by Bea Kopp*

A Peninsula institution came to an end when the Old Bay Line steamboat *City of Richmond* made her final call at Old Point Comfort, December 30, 1959.

The boat sailed daily between Norfolk and Baltimore with a Peninsula stop at Old Point Comfort, continuing the tradition of providing Lower Peninsula residents with essential transportation.

The Old Bay Line, founded in 1840, was the oldest continuous passenger and freight service in existence when it went out of service in 1962, a victim of the automobile era.

And the *City of Richmond?* Built in 1913 in Baltimore, she was scheduled to be towed to the Virgin Islands in 1964 to be converted into a floating resort hotel, restaurant and nightclub. But perhaps unhappy about her new role, she sank during the trip south.

*Photo by Alexander C. Brown*

An aerial view of Newport News' port facilities and Newport News Shipbuilding in the background.

*Courtesy of The Daily Press, Inc.*

The C & O docking tug *George W. Stevens* and the Greek collier *Theonymphos* were at the coal piers in Newport News in February 1964. Since Hampton's prominence as a port in the 1700's, cargo ships have been a familiar site at the Lower Peninsula. Since the beginning of Newport News, the city has become a major port on the East Coast.

*Photo by Alexander C. Brown*

THEONYMPHOS

An icy day on the Peninsula in 1967.

*Photo by Bea Kopp*

Ray Charles is one of many jazz luminaries who have trouped to the Peninsula to participate in the annual Hampton Jazz Festival.

Begun in 1968 at Hampton Institute, the first three-day festival attracted some 25,000 people. In 1970 the event was moved to Hampton Coliseum.

The festival has received national recognition and has been praised for bringing the entire community together in an undertaking of cultural and social value.

*Photo by Bea Kopp*

Although this appears to be a moon landing, it's astronaut Edwin Aldrin maneuvering a lunar landing module at NASA, Langley Research Center, in June 1969. The astronaut was simulating touchdown on the moon, training which paid off a month later when he and astronaut Neil A. Armstrong landed on the real thing instead of this concrete and slag reproduction of the lunar surface.

This training is just one of the many contributions made by Langley scientists to the success of the Apollo mission and its "giant leap for mankind."

*Photo by Jim Livengood*
*Courtesy of The Daily Press, Inc.*

Resembling a jewel in a crown, Hampton Coliseum officially opened January 31, 1970. Located on a seventy-five acre tract adjacent to Interstate 64, the architecturally unique hall cost $8.5 million, but it has given the area a gorgeous and flexible setting for various types of entertainment. Basketball, ice skating and other sports are regularly scheduled at the coliseum. Musical events such as rock concerts and symphony orchestra performances are held there throughout the year.

*Photo by Jim Livengood*
*Courtesy of The Daily Press, Inc.*

Although the Hampton Coliseum offically opened in January 1970, a basketball game between the College of William and Mary and North Carolina State on December 1, 1969, was the first event to be scheduled in the facility. Workmen put finishing touches on the court the afternoon of the game.

*Courtesy of The Daily Press, Inc.*

Hampton Mayor Ann Kilgore presents "39-year-old" comedian Jack Benny with a key to the Hampton vault at the Hampton Coliseum dedication ceremony January 31, 1970. Benny entertained dignitaries and about 9,000 people at the Saturday night opening.

*Photo by Jim Livengood*
*Courtesy of The Daily Press, Inc.*

Some people have all the luck. In this case it's Bob Hope, guest star of the Miss World-U.S.A. Beauty Pageant sponsored by the City of Hampton at the Hampton Roads Coliseum. Hope is congratulating Miss Lynda Carter (Miss Arizona-World), who has just been crowned Miss World-U.S.A. during the September 1, 1972, pageant. Hope and the winner are flanked by lovely runners-up and David Janssen, one of the judges. The contest was the second pageant hosted by Hampton, but the city declined to sponsor the event after the second year.

*Photo by Bea Kopp*

Hampton Association for the Arts and Humanities has conducted historical and archeaological research in Old Hampton in cooperation with the Hampton Redevelopment and Housing Authority since 1967. Excavated in 1970, this well was on the property of Moss Wallace Armistead.

Armistead, one of Hampton's leading merchants at the time of the Revolutionary War, was the first postmaster for the town. The site is now part of Hampton's Heritage Park.

*Courtesy of Hampton Association for the Arts and Humanities*

Ship launchings have brought a steady stream of dignitaries to Newport News Shipbuilding to try their luck at smashing champagne bottles. In 1971, Mrs. Richard Nixon smashes a bottle on the guided missile frigate *USS California* as former Newport News Shipbuilding president L.C. Ackerman observes her determined efforts.

*Photo by Bea Kopp*

This serene view of Newport Towers, taken from Christopher Newport Park, shows the 15-story luxury apartment building which opened in January 1973 on West Avenue and 28th Street. Designed by Max Ratner, a Cleveland architect, it is an important element in Newport News' efforts to revitalize the downtown area.

*Photo by Bea Kopp*

Buckroe Beach in June 1974.

*Courtesy of The Daily Press, Inc.*

A resort beach without sand spells trouble; like Virginia Beach, Buckroe is periodically concerned with retaining sand. In this method, a scooper shovels sand out of salt water ponds and deposits it along the shoreline. This striking view on a cloudy day makes work seem artistic.

*Photo by Ransy Morr*
*Courtesy of The Daily Press, Inc.*

A host of dignitaries, including Virginia Governor Mills E. Godwin, Jr. and Secretary of the Navy J. William Middendorf, and a tremendous crowd attend the launching of the *USS Virginia* on December 14, 1974, at Newport News Shipbuilding. The nuclear cruiser is an awesome sight.

*Photo by Bea Kopp*

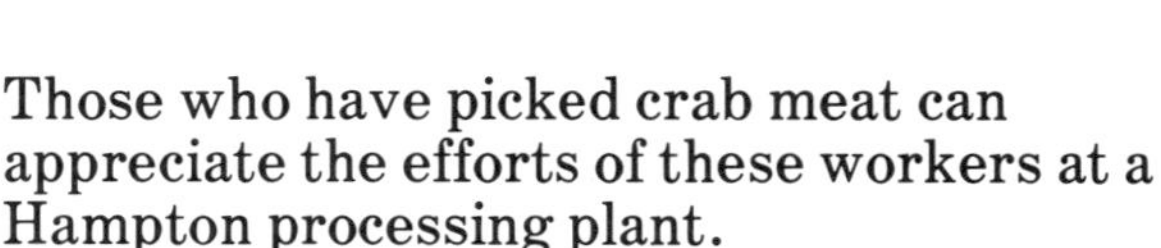

Those who have picked crab meat can appreciate the efforts of these workers at a Hampton processing plant.

*Photo by Bea Kopp*

In January 1975, Newport News Shipbuilding's Goliath Gantry crane went into operation. With a lift capacity of 900 tons, the crane can serve over twenty-two acres. The 234-foot-high crane completely dominates this view of the north yard.

*Photo by Jim Livengood*
*Courtesy of The Daily Press, Inc.*

Anyone who has ever had a hair-raising ride over the James River Bridge will consider the completion of the new trestle a noteworthy achievement in Peninsula history.

Begun in early 1973, the modern span was opened in April and June of 1975. These aerial views show the center section and the trestle that begins on the Peninsula.

*Photos by Jim Livengood*
*Courtesy of The Daily Press, Inc.*

The Hampton Veterans Administration Center began in 1855 as the Chesapeake Female Seminary to educate young Virginia women. It was part of Camp Hamilton during the Civil War.

The federal government purchased the property in 1870 for the Southern Branch of the National Asylum for Disabled Volunteer Soldiers. When the asylum opened, there was a hospital and dormitory, which had been the main building of the seminary. In 1873, the name was changed to Southern Branch of the National Home for Disabled Volunteer Soldiers.

The facility underwent several expansions, particularly in 1885 and 1897. In 1899, a crisis developed. Yellow fever spread through the soldiers' home and eventually to Phoebus. A strict quarantine was established to stop the spread of the disease, but twenty-two of the soldiers died before the fever was controlled.

In 1930 the home became the Kecoughtan, and later Hampton, Veterans Administration.

*Photo by Bea Kopp*

A contemporary view of a sport that has been popular throughout the history of the Lower Peninsula. Although somewhat limited in its appeal, fox hunting still maintains a dedicated following.

*Photo by Bea Kopp*

Sailing in the 1970's.

*Photo by Bea Kopp*

Harrison Phoebus' once elegant Roseland Manor, built in 1886, was the pride of Phoebus. But the mansion he built for his family, now the Manor House of Strawberry Banks Motel, only hints at its original grandeur in this contemporary view.

*Photo by Bea Kopp*

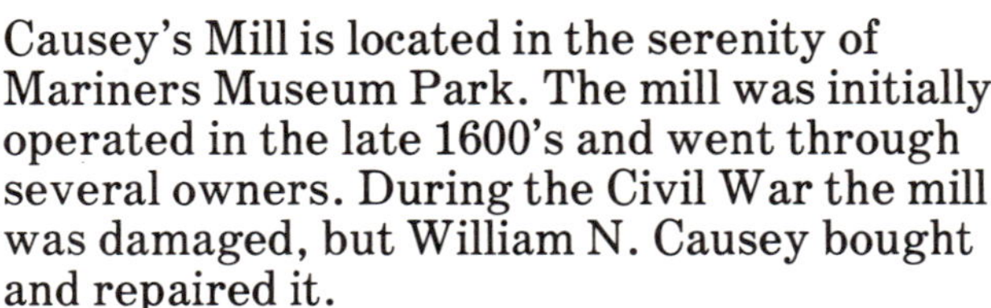

Causey's Mill is located in the serenity of Mariners Museum Park. The mill was initially operated in the late 1600's and went through several owners. During the Civil War the mill was damaged, but William N. Causey bought and repaired it.

*Photo by Bea Kopp*

Leonard's Saloon and Ladies & Gents Cafe For White People Only was discovered in March 1975 as construction workers cleared old buildings on the southeast corner of Queen and King streets in Hampton to make way for the United Virginia C & M Bank.

Leonard's Saloon helped quench the thirst of Hampton citizens until prohibition.

*Photo by Ransy Morr*
*Courtesy of The Daily Press, Inc.*

The Lower Peninsula is riding the shopping wave of the future with the completion of two giant malls in the 1970's. Located on Mercury Boulevard, Coliseum Mall opened in October 1973, and Newmarket North opened in March 1975.

Following a trend that has taken hold throughout the country, the malls have both major retailers and specialty shops under the same roof.

These photographs show Coliseum Mall (Korvettes) and Newmarket North (Sears).

*Photos by Bea Kopp*

These small stores are an anachronism on Mercury Boulevard in 1975, just across the boulevard from the giant Newmarket North shopping mall.

*Photo by Bea Kopp*

Today the Virginia National Bank building is located on the corner of Hampton's historic King and Queen streets. Built in 1970, the building provides a view of things to come in the city.

The citizens and Hampton Redevelopment and Housing Authority, created in the late 1950's, have joined hands to renew the city in a way that will maintain the Colonial flavor, which is enhanced by antique gaslights imported from Manchester, England.

With an emphasis on the needs of people, the citizens of Hampton are working to maintain the best of the past for the people of the future.

*Photos by Bea Kopp*

HOTEL WARWICK

This modern view of Newport News serves as a vivid contrast between the old city and the new. The Victory Arch and Hotel Warwick represent the past, and the new city hall in the background is a symbol of the future.

Newport News Redevelopment and Housing Authority, established around 1940, is working with the city to encourage citizen participation and to achieve rehabilitation and conservation of the city. It is hoped that the efforts of organizations and individuals will achieve productive results for the greatest number of people.

*Photo by Bea Kopp*

Hampton Coliseum on a foggy night resembles some ethereal spaceship or flying saucer. Two late arrivals for a musical performance walking across the rain-soaked parking lot add to the eerie effect.

*Photo by Tom Slater*
*Courtesy of The Daily Press, Inc.*

# ACKNOWLEDGEMENTS

It is no exaggeration to say this book could not have been completed without the help of Bea Kopp. She worked under severe time restrictions, and with old photographs that were extremely difficult to copy, to produce pictures of the highest possible quality. Bea also took most of the modern photographs, and I think her work speaks for itself.

The list of people who provided invaluable assistance is much to long to print here, but I must thank Alexander C. Brown, Mrs. Sandidge Evans and John Mitchell, who read the manuscript for accuracy.

I also owe a tremendous debt to all the organizations and people who provided photographs for this pictorial history. The people who work at the military bases, museums and libraries were wonderfully cooperative.

And I want to thank my wife Ruth who encouraged me throughout the work and, as usual, provided a helping hand when I needed it most.

*Photo by Bea Kopp*

# BIBLIOGRAPHY

Alexander, Edward P. *The Journal of John Fontaine.* Colonial Williamsburg, 1972.

Arthur, Robert. *History of Fort Monroe.* Fort Monroe: The Coast Artillery School Press, 1930.

Jester, Annie Lash. *Newport News, Virginia, 1607-1960.* City of Newport News, 1961.

McCabe, Gillie Cary. *The Story of an Old Town -- Hampton, Virginia.* Richmond: Old Dominion Press, 1929.

Rankin, Hugh F. *The Golden Age of Piracy.* Colonial Williamsburg. Distributed by Holt, Rinehart and Winston, Inc., New York, 1969.

Rouse, Park, Jr. *Endless Harbor. The Story of Newport News.* City of Newport News, Virginia, 1969.

Sinclair, Margaret Munford. *In and Around Hampton.* 1957.

Stanard, Mary Newton. *Colonial Virginia. Its People and Customs.* Detroit: Singing Tree Press, 1970.

Starkey, Marion L. *The First Plantation. History of Hampton and Elizabeth City County, Virginia. 1607-1887.* Hampton: Houston Printing and Publishing House, 1936.

*Tales of Old Fort Monroe.* A series of monographs published by the Committee for the Fort Monroe Casemate Museum, Newport News.

Taylor, Donald Ransome. *Out of the Past -- the Future: A History of Hampton, Virginia.* Hampton: Prestige Press, Inc., 1960.

Thane, Elswyth. *The Virginia Colony.* London: Crowell-Collier Press, Collier-Macmillan Ltd., 1969.

White, William Chapman and Ruth White. *Tin Can on a Shingle.* New York: E.P. Dutton & Co., Inc., 1957.